Make Her Chase You: The Simple Strategy to Attract Women

Copyright Notice

Darcy Carter 2018

Buyer Bonus

I want to thank you for your purchase of this book. As a way of extending my thanks I am giving you full access to exclusive resources, including:

- Free courses and books
- Building a lifestyle that will guarantee you success with women
- How to Look and Feel Your Best
- Keep the conversation going, without appearing awkward
- How to confidently express yourself and captivate attention
- And much more about confidence, relationships and dating

Free Sign Up Here

About the Author

Would you believe me if I tell you that someone who has zero self-confidence and is shy around girls can transform into an alpha male who attracts all kinds of women anywhere he goes? You better believe it because I am a living and breathing testimony that this can happen.

Let me tell you my story is so similar to the ugly duckling but with a lot more interesting events and plot twists. You would think the author of this famous children's tale was making a reference to my life story.

Growing up, I was a shy, awkward boy with very few friends. I had crushes but I didn't really do anything about them because of my shyness. I didn't know how to talk to girls my age. I wasn't a particularly bad looking kid, just one who didn't know how to be cool or fit in with the others. Girls were interested in me now and then but I was lost for words and not knowing what to do they often left me.

After high school I was still lonely and lacking a lot of experience compared to my friends. With high hopes of finding love, I left home and went to university. I was still a shy student, especially since it was a new place with new people. Most of the time I kept to myself because it felt more comfortable being this way. I only had two or three guy friends to hang out with.

During this time I noticed some older exchange students would always be approaching girls and seemed to have massive confidence even if they were rejected. This inspired me with some confidence and I talked to a few girls on the university campus. The results were mixed but I was still pretty shy and I didn't follow a system so my success rate in the dating scene was pitiful.

Luckily some girls accepted me but I felt like a fake, and I knew at the time that these girls just needed something from me--a ride somewhere or help with a particularly difficult paper or project. I knew it, but I let them because what was I supposed to do? Guys like me didn't have any choice. I was always putting them way up in my mind, that they were out of my reach and they were just accepting me because they felt sorry for me. Believing this made it a reality and it projected my low self esteem onto them.

After a few short relationships which did not go further because of my lack of skills I met Emily. I was 22 years old at the time and had never been in a proper relationship. Sure I had crushes, slept with a few girls and had dated a few, but no one compared to Emily. She was the love of my life. I met her at house party and we hit if off right away.

Things went well at first, we saw each other a few times a week and we had fallen in love. Gradually I began to take her for granted and I let myself go. She became my world. I stopped seeing my friends. I stopped working out and buying new clothes. I even grew my hair long!

When university was over it was time for us to go back to our parents. I had become dependent on her and couldn't be without her so I asked her to move in with me and my parents. That was a bad idea!

Things were great at first but after some time, she became busy with her new job. In the meantime I was unemployed and figuring out my next move. For me things weren't going anywhere and it turned me into a clingy boyfriend who always needed to know where she was and what she was doing. I don't know why but maybe because I knew deep down that she could have someone a lot better than myself. I felt insecure and jealous all the time, until she became fed up, and left me. I was devastated and I thought I wouldn't be able to move on. I was lost for a year, other girls didn't interest me. Emily was my world and without her my life lacked meaning. We got back together a few times but it never worked out.

The truth was I knew deep down we were not meant for eachother and i was just afraid of the unknown, of going out on my path as a man. At the back of my mind I felt like there was a whole dating world that was out there to explore. But I knew it would be difficult for me to go back to the dating scene and try my luck again. Afterall, I was unlucky in love considering my past experiences with women.

One lonely day in amongst a block of many lonely days I came across some websites about how to meet girls. I found out that there were average men like me were using proven dating strategies to consistently hook up with quality women whenever they wanted. These guys were going out day and night meeting women and hooking up with them, sometimes multiple women at a time!

I was hooked in and devoured everything I could on this subject. I met some new male friends from online and observed how they effortlessly attracted women around them. During this time I even hired a dating coach, he took me out to some bars and I tried what he taught me. I observed, studied, took notes, and decided to give it a shot. I had nothing to lose anyway. If there is one thing that I regret about my life, it's not knowing about these techniques earlier on.

From there on I gained experience in attracting and wooing women the right away. My first steps were timid, I was so shy. Asking for directions from a random woman on the street or even smiling at a girl in a club was a massive mental effort for me. Overcoming the anxiety was my biggest hurdle.

Nowadays, I have dates with the hottest women in town left and right. I have dated corporate types, budding actresses, models, doctors, business owners, singers, and many more. Now I can choose whoever I like, when not long before I had to settle for whoever came along. Mind you, I didn't do anything too drastic and expensive, like undergoing plastic surgery or buying a sports car or mansion to impress the ladies. I just tweaked my personality and lifestyle a tiny bit. Okay....,not a tiny bit but you get what I mean. I didn't have to do the impossible. My solution is something that anyone can do.

And the good news is I decided to compile everything and write a book about it. You might ask why I am doing this. The answer is simple. I want to help guys who are just like my old self--shy and awkward with low self-esteem.

Maybe it is my mission in life, to be the fairy godfather of these guys who cannot seem to find luck in dating and transform them into attractive males by letting them in on the secret.

You probably belong to this group of guys if you are reading this. If so, sit back, learn, and get ready to experience a major overhaul that will turn you into a man that every woman wants to meet and be with.

Contents

Chapter 1: The Perfect Girl

In dating, it takes two to tango. Cliché but oh so true. It is never one-sided. Just because you found the girl that you think you want to marry, or at least you want to "Netflix and chill" with, does not mean that's the end of the story. You also need to be the kind of man that women are attracted to. Sure, you might have found your dream girl who looks like Cara Delevingne, is a successful business owner, and plays the piano but what about you? What can you offer in return?

Let's tackle this one by one. First, you need to identify the kind of girl that you want to go home with, want to date, or want to marry. Whatever your ultimate goal is. You need to have a clear picture in your head, not just her looks (which is not really that important in the long run, to be completely honest) but also what she does and who she is as a person. By defining what you want in a woman you will cut straight to the chase and attract what you want.

Here are some guidelines that will help you identify the kind of women you want to meet.

Age

First things first. Do you have a specific age group in mind? Some men are attracted to younger women (but not young as in minor, please) while others are attracted to women who are older. There are also men who prefer women who are of the same age as them.

There are varying reasons for this. I have met men who are attracted to women who are a lot younger because they feel like they want to be the provider and protector of these young ladies. Nothing wrong there, as long as she is legal. I also have male friends who are into women that are five to six years their senior, simply because they love women who are sophisticated and experienced. The majority of the men I know want to meet women who are the same age or at least two to three years their junior. Their reason is because they want to be with someone who they can consider their equal. However, there is no right age group when it comes to dating because it all depends on your preference.

Women are often attracted to older men as they prefer stability and maturity. Younger guys often are attracted to older women as they find experience a turn on. In each situation you need to adapt. When attracting older women you should be well balanced, respectful and a renaissance kind of man who is well cultured and experienced. Older women value these traits in a man. For attracting younger women you should act as a provider of security, comfort and wisdom. Maintain your youth and vitality by staying in shape and in tune with good fashion sense and awareness of trends.

Beauty

Although personality goes a long way when it comes to building a relationship with someone, beauty definitely is an important factor, especially when meeting women for the first time. The first thing that attracts you to a woman is her appearance because you cannot determine a woman's personality without interacting with her first. And in some people, it may take longer to get to know them. So initial attraction between two people is usually based on appearance. Everyone wants to date someone who is beautiful, just keep in mind that this should not be your sole deciding factor when looking for someone to be your girlfriend. Although physical attractiveness is enough if you are just after hooking up or for a one night stand.

Beautiful women receive a lot of attention from men. You need to stand out from the crowd. How can you do that? Stay grounded when you are with her, don't get lost in her beauty or hang off her every word. Express yourself, tell her what you like and don't like. Challenge her responses to your questions. Set the frame that you are the man and she is the woman. You lead and she follows. You don't need to be an arrogant jerk, be a gentleman at the same time and show empathy for her emotions. For her, being with you should feel like a rollercoaster of romantic emotions. You are at the center of it all, her rock in the waves.

Regarding beauty, ask yourself questions such as. Do you like brunettes, blondes, asians? How beautiful should she be, does she look great naturally or is she a botox queen?

Smart

Nobody wants to date a bimbo or someone who's lacking in the brain department because it will get boring fast. Although this does not really matter if you are just looking for someone to hook up with. Believe it or not, there are some men who like to date airheads because it makes them feel superior but don't be like this kind of man. You want to date someone who can hold her end of the conversation without any problem. She does not necessarily have to have a PhD or be a rocket scientist. Although it's also fine if that's what you want. As long as she knows basic stuff and is up to date with what's happening around her, she'd be fine. It's all your choice

When interacting with an intelligent woman, you need to be prepared to have intelligent conversations that do not just revolve around the weather or gossip. You need to match her intelligence not in the literal sense, as in you do not really need to know everything about biotechnology if she is into that kind of stuff. Asking intelligent questions and being simply knowledgeable about a variety of topics will go a long way. You can read up on current events online or watch news and always be learning about things. Practicing talking with smart people in daily life and having intelligent friends with help you. Men who love to read are very attractive to these types of women, so if you are not an avid reader, you should start to become one. You can start by reading classic books that you can insert while having conversations with these types of women.

A word of advice, if you don't know about a subject then don't claim to know about it. When she starts asking you questions about it or talking in details you will look a fool. It's better to be honest and take an interest in any new subjects.

Women who are considered as intelligent can often be found in libraries, bookstores (surprise, surprise), conferences, courses or coffee shops for example. Make sure you approach them in a polite way and have a frame of mind to offer value and intellectually, stimulating conversation.

Healthy

I have yet to meet a man who is actively seeking a woman who is sickly or has an illness. Of course, men want to date women who are healthy! Healthy women have great bodies because they always work out and eat balanced meals. They are also fun to be with and can do most physical activities because they are in great shape. Being fit also makes sex great!

On the other hand, there are those women who are obsessed about their weight. And you should not confuse these with healthy women because there is a big difference. A healthy woman will treat herself to a slice of cake or an ice cream from time to time but a woman who is obsessed about her weight will always say no to such treats. It is no fun to date a weight-obsessed woman because all she will ever think about is her weight. Plus, it would be a nightmare to take her out for dinner.

And how can you find a healthy woman if you are not healthy yourself? You first need to improve not only your health but also the way you carry yourself. Slouching and frowning will make you look like you are not in great shape. Always sit and stand straight and put a smile on your face. And it goes without saying, always exercise and eat healthy. Healthy women who are looking for men like them will not be attracted to someone who has a beer belly or who smokes, so quit your bad habits before you go out and approach these women.

Healthy women are often found working out at the gym, jogging outside, eating at a vegan restaurant, or shopping at Trader Joe's or Whole Foods. A great way to meet them is to attend exercise classes such as yoga or dancing. These classes are full of women, you will usually be the only guy there. Or at least the only straight guy! Don't be shy to look a fool if you have no experience in the class, women will love teaching you and it will provide great opportunities to open the conversation. You can also utilize this at the gym. Help a girl lifting weights and give her advice on technique. Be smooth and confident and avoid being a creepy stalker.

Funny

If you want a woman who has a sense of humor, you are one of the millions of men who want the same thing. Men find funny girls sexy and confident. After all, you cannot crack jokes or laugh at yourself if you do not have high self-esteem. Funny women are fun to be with, obviously. Being with her is always full of laughter. But keep in mind that you might find it more difficult to steer your conversation to something more serious and intimate if you are always laughing. When you find a break from all the laughing and joking, you can start a more serious and intimate conversation with her.

Funny women are also intelligent but in a light-hearted kind of way, unlike the intelligent types who are into neuroscience or quantum physics. You can match their humor by not being too serious all the time. Make her laugh at things in the environment you are in. Tell her stories that are funny, make fun of her. One word of caution, though, is to not be funny at the expense of others. Do not ever make fun of other people just to make her laugh. Chances are she will not appreciate that kind of humor and she will find you mean and douchey. Also avoid politically sensitive topics, gender roles, racism or nationalism. Some girls might be offended by making fun of these topics and she might not tell you then, but later she will disappear.

Humour is a potent seduction tool so if you can master it then your romantic success will sky rocket. It's no secret that comedians get laid like crazy, look at Eddie Murphy or Russell Brand. You can become more funny by observing the great stand up comedians and funny movies. Figure out what makes them funny and add it to your personality.

Funny women are everywhere, and you will usually find them with a group of friends because they love their audience. There are also quiet women who are funny when you get to talk to them and they feel comfortable enough to show their real side. It's all about approaching them in a non threatening way and building comfort with humour.

Reliable

This is a difficult trait to gauge especially when you just met for the first time. But you can check for telltale signs if someone is reliable. For instance, if she has a regular stable job and is supporting herself without any problem, she is most likely a reliable person. Another sign is if she does not get herself too drunk while she is out with friends, which means she wants to be in her right frame of mind when in public. If you see her outside babysitting children or walking several dogs in the park, she is probably reliable because she can be trusted with small children and pets. You cannot really tell the first time you talk to her but you can definitely search for clues that will give you an idea if she is a reliable person.

If you want a woman who is reliable, maybe someone who is working and earning money for herself, then you should also be a reliable man who supports himself. It is just too embarrassing if you are still living in your parents' house because you do not have a job. Be the man who is in control of his life.

You can find reliable women in classes, the library, or seminars. Remember not to judge women who enjoy going to the bar as unreliable. They probably just want to have fun so be in the lookout even in these kinds of places also.

Honest

Who doesn't want an honest person even just to be friends with? Even more so if you want to date that person. However, this is probably even more difficult to tell on the first meetup because how can you tell if someone is not being honest, unless they flat out tell a lie? The trick here is to pay attention to what she is saying and notice those things that do not match. Remember, you can catch a liar in her own web of lies. She might forget her story because she is not telling the truth. Another way to tell if she is not an honest person is by simply observing. If she mentions in passing that she dated two guys at the same time in the past, it is possible that she might do this again in her future relationships. Or something as simple as exaggerating things just to make herself look more interesting can be a sign of dishonesty. Stay away from this type of woman because they will only cause you trouble and heartache.

To attract women who are honest, you should also be honest about yourself. Do not pretend to be someone you are not just to impress a girl because you will get caught sooner or later. Believe me, I tried this before. I pretended to have a read a book that a girl I like asked about and I ended up looking like a fool because it was her favorite book and she was so excited to find someone who likes it as well, only to realize that I was lying after saying vague and generic replies to her over enthusiastic questions about the book. These women can see through your pickup lines and will immediately know that you are talking to her because you are attracted to her.

Honest women are everywhere. All you need to do is look. When approaching them, just be straightforward and don't play any games. If you set the right frame from the start by being honest with them about everything, including your intentions then it should be smooth sailing. If you feel she is dishonest then leave.

Respectable

In this time and age of modern dating, of swiping left or right in Tinder, of inviting someone to just Netflix and chill, of simply wanting to hookup, can you still find a respectable woman who values herself? Yes, of course. There are still plenty of women who respect themselves and who do not act in slutty ways. It is easy to find respectable women by simply looking at them. It is not just what they are wearing, but how they behave. Drinking too much and dirty dancing with just about any men on the dance floor can be considered slutty. Making out with a man she just met three seconds ago is not the behavior of a respectable woman. Someone who is respectable carries herself with quiet dignity. And is not loud or obnoxious. She has class and sophistication that a lot of men find really attractive.

Respectable women have a high standard when it comes to men. They want men who they can be proud of. Having a regular stable job is a sign of respectability because you are working your ass off to support yourself without the help of others. You also need to be respectful with not only women but other people around you. During your day to day life treat people with respect. Open doors for people, help others when they are in need and be polite to everyone. Being respectful and being respectable may not be the same but they surely go hand in hand. If your a respectable gentleman then approaching women in a polite way will quickly help you identify like minded women. Because anyone who reacts negatively to politeness is not worthy of your time. Don't engage in their negativity just walk away with your head held high.

Respectable women can also be found anywhere, even in clubs and bars. You will just see them in the sidelines, quietly sipping on their cocktail drinks and simply observing people around them. They do not want to make a fool of themselves so they do not drink beyond their capacity.

Sexy

Being sexy is a lot more than having the perfect body figure. It is also about the way she carries herself, her intelligence, and also her confidence. Do you want to date someone who is sexy? Of course, you do! Just like every man I have ever met. Someone who is sexy knows what she wants and goes after what she wants. She also knows what she can offer. Sexy is also having a figure that all women want to have and men lust after. She can wear the most conservative outfit but still exude sex appeal because of the way she carries herself.

If you want to meet someone like this, be prepared to lose your mind! Just kidding....Be prepared to be the kind of man who can handle all of this sexiness. You need to be confident about yourself and not be insecure because these women can attract all kinds of men. You will have a lot of competition and if you want to win, you need to have an edge over all of them. This kind of woman is the female version of the alpha male. Or the alpha female (duh). You need to become the alpha male if you want to conquer the alpha female because otherwise, you do not stand a chance. Act cool and confident at all times, especially when she tests you or your are together in a stressful situation.

You can find these magnificent creatures anywhere. Be ready! You will notice them a mile away because they ooze confidence and sex appeal. You will also notice a lot of men eyeing her. But only a few will make a move because most will be intimidated, thinking that she is just beyond their reach. This should be you. You are an alpha male, and you can definitely go up to her and start a conversation, and ultimately, take her home with you.

You might be attracted to other traits and personalities that are not included in this list. If there are other traits you think are important to you, then list them. Go into detail. What is her eye color? What is her body type? Does she smoke? Is she popular? Whatever is important to you list it. Then keep that description of your ideal woman in your mind, refresh it daily by looking at it. This will bring it into your awareness. Having a clear picture of the woman you want will help you to have a better understanding of where to find your type of girl, what kind of man you need to become and how to behave with her. The most important thing is that you know what you want and you do what it takes to win her heart.

In the following chapter you will learn some helpful tips that will improve as a man and become the guy that every woman wants to be with.

Chapter 2: How to be Attractive

One cannot simply become an attractive man without making an effort to be one. Sure, some guys are born with good looks and confidence but that is not the only requirement. There is much more. You need to know the secrets that these men have so that you can become like them.

The first principle that you need to know is to **be consistent and persistent**. If you are consistent and persistent in the dating game, then it will keep you young. What does that mean? It does not mean you remain young with age, but it means a number of other things. For one, if you are an active participant in the dating game, your techniques are more in tune with the current scene no matter how old you are. Dating and being single is journey that requires self observation, action and constant self improvement. if you are actively consistent and persistent when the going gets tough it will result in a lifetime of dating abundance, use the force with care!

Let's take a look at two guys who are both in their mid-30s who are currently single and are out looking for fun dates. You have one guy who has been dating continuously year after year with persistence, working on improving himself. The other guy who's a bit rusty because he hasn't been in the dating scene for years and has been relatively inconsistent with his romantic life. When the going got tough he gave up or got distracted with work. Guy one will have an idea about the modern aspects of dating such as creating an effective profile on Tinder or knowing what "Netflix and chill means". Guy two would probably have an idea what Tinder means but would not know how to use the app and "Netflix and chill" for him probably means literally what it means--watching Netflix and hanging out.

In this scenario, guy one will have a bigger chance at getting dates because he knows how it works these days. After all, he is consistently dating and he will know how dating strategies evolve through time and how he can use this knowledge to his advantage. And because he knows the ways of the modern dating scene, he will appear youthful to a lot of women. He knows that rejection does not mean failure. He believes in abundance, just because one door is close another will be open.

Women do not want to feel like they are dating their father or grandfather because of the way you interact with them. Besides, how can you become an alpha male if you do not go out there and mingle not only with the women that you are trying to win but also with the other guys who will become your competitors? Staying in the game keeps you on your toes, keeps you fit, maintains your appearance and gives you life satisfaction. Even if you are in a relationship it doesn't mean that you let yourself go. Stay in the game and keep the fire in your relationship by applying the skill set to your girl.

Go for Quality

Aside from being consistent in the dating game you must always go for quality. In turn you will become "quality" yourself. How does this work? First, let's understand what "going for quality" means. This does not mean discriminating women just because they do not look like a celebrity or they do not work in a big company. Being choosy like this will leave you dateless and make you come off as obnoxious. Treat others as you wish to be treated.

Going for quality simply means targeting women that meet your standards. If you like really hot girls, or smart girls, then go for them. It doesn't mean ignore everyone else, you can be friends with them. But when it comes to dating, never drop your standards. After all, why would you exert an effort on someone when you know it won't lead to a serious relationship? Unless of course you are just looking for a hookup.

If you are in your 30s and you are looking for someone your age, why would you waste your time and effort trying to win college students when you know you are looking for something else and the wrong age is a deal breaker for you? Do not go after all women that you see just because you are trying to increase the chances of securing dates. This is not the lottery! Be selective.

When you apply this principle it will elevate your life because when you raise the bar you must hone your dating strategies and skills. Interacting with these high quality women will give you an idea of what is attractive and not attractive for them. The saying "practice makes perfect "is applicable in this situation. Constantly strive to become better, it is the solution to every challenge.

However don't be a jerk and ignore friendly girls just because you don't fancy them. Sure, you should not actively pursue women that you are not interested in. But you should definitely make them feel interesting and attractive when they initiate a conversation with you. One of the keys of becoming a better seducer is to flirt with any women who come your way. This will make you a more sociable and likeable person.

Always On

Be ready for whatever. If a pretty girl walks past you, talk, no excuses. By always being social and cheerful in your neighbourhood and your life it will make you more attractive and get you out of your head. Sometimes those interactions don't go anywhere but sometimes a five minute conversation can turn into years of love, sex and happiness.

Make sure you are calibrated to the situation or environment you are in. You don't want to be super loud in a library or flirt too much on the subway as examples.

Treat all girls the same

Do not be intimidated to flirt with women who come from a completely different socio-economic background, are super hot, or with women from a different race. Do not think they are out of your reach or are too mysterious to even try. Just talk to them and flirt with them and you will see that all women want from a man, no matter who she is or where she came from, is to make her feel attractive and interesting. Flirt with them just for the sake of flirting and without any hidden agenda or motive, and you will be rewarded even more by the female population. Just you wait and see.

Another important principle is to **be flexible** to anything, whether it is beneficial to you right now or in the long run. Women change more than the English weather. They will often subconsciously test you. Maybe you are looking for a serious relationship and a woman says she is not interested in a long-term relationship right now. That does not mean you should stop talking to her. You can still continue to hang out with her, maybe even hook up with her. Who knows, she might just change her mind, fall for you, chase you and decide that she wants to have a serious relationship with you. This is something that you should definitely do if you are extremely attracted to the girl. Remember that in dating, and just about any other aspect in life, patience is a virtue.

You should also be flexible to the environments you are in. For example maybe you are out clubbing and guys keep hitting on your girl. Be flexible and don't try to control the situation. If your girl is truly into you and is worth your time then she will brush them off. Be flexible anytime with your girl, sometimes things won't go to plan and you need to adapt. I remember being on a date and the place we planned to go was fully booked. This led to a location change were we ended up in a nice intimate bar that was way better than the crowded one before. Turn the negatives into positives.

Never Give Up

When things are not going according to plan or if you are in unfamiliar territory. If you have just moved to a new place or you are trying out a new strategy, you will experience a decrease in your success rate. Maybe you went out and got rejected all night or your date flaked on you. But remember that this will not last long. The real man gets back up when he is knocked down.

Surround yourself with positive people and have an interesting life so you can ride out the rough times. On the grand scheme of things it will all be worth the effort. Focus on the journey and not the destination. Again, patience is a virtue in the dating world.

To summarize the major points:

1. **Be consistent**
2. **Go for quality**
3. **Always on**
4. **Treat all girls the same**
5. **Be Flexible**
6. **Never give up**

These principles apply to all kinds of dating scenarios and to all people of different ages and backgrounds. Whatever level your coming from can't be much worse than I was. Believe me it works! Focus on the key skills and elevate your life to the next level.

In the next chapter there are some great tools and mindsets to help you become a more attractive man and master your life and psychology.

Chapter 3: Make Her Chase You

Mastering your inner game is the key to make women want you. What is inner game? It is all about how you feel about yourself, and your lifestyle manifested. Your inner game is just as important as your outer game (outer game is the dating strategy that you use to attract your target females). Work on yourself and the women will be drawn to you.

To give you a better idea, my inner game issue was to change my boring job to something more exciting, that brings me closer to ladies, and pays more. I followed my dreams and became a DJ. My family thought I was out of my mind because never in their entire lives did they think that I would become a DJ. But here I am, and I am loving every minute of it. Not just because of the ladies (although that's a big factor) but also because I really love what I am doing now. Not only it is not only a cool job that helps me meet ladies but it also pays well especially once you have connections. I have the opportunity to travel the world, plus I get perks like tickets to events and concerts which I share with family and friends.

It is important to note that if you change, you do it not only for the sake of attracting women but also because it is something that you really want for yourself. This will give you more confidence because you will be on your path towards doing what you love. In turn it will be reflected in your outward life. Maybe you are not in an attractive job. But if it's your passion, be proud of what you do and stay committed to your job. If it's something you are not passionate about, make steps towards changes. Change location, learn and take responsibility for your life. Your the only one who will. Someone who loves his job and is proud of it is also a plus in women's books because they do not want to be with whiners who always complain about his workload or his boss.

Some men may also be guilty of burying themselves in work and avoiding the dating life thanks to illusionary excuses. Of course we all need to make money, live the dream and be successful. But don't neglect your love life and be one of those old guys at the pub who fell in love with football as a distraction from his loneliness. As they say, all work and no play makes Jack a dull boy.

But going back to dating, what are the things that you need to do to become an attractive male? Attractive males have certain qualities about them that set them apart from ordinary guys. How do you feel about yourself and how does that reflect into the world?

The first thing is to **know the kind of self-image that you wish to portray,** in this case, you want people to see you as someone who has self-confidence and can get any woman he sets his eyes on. To be able to make people see you like this, you first need to see yourself, the way you want others to see you. But how? Well, you need to feel it inside you!

You have probably heard of athletes talking about their game, when they can see nothing else but the ball in slow motion, and everything else—the audience and opponent—is not part of the picture. They can feel their talent, strength, and skill as they go towards the ball. They are "in the zone" and nothing else matters but achieving the goal. This is what alpha males feel when they talk to women that they are attracted to. They only see their target—the woman—and everything else is a blur. And the women, and even men, can feel this sense of power and confidence. This confidence is what makes a man an alpha male. Women flock all over them and men look up to them for advice or guidance and want to be on their good side.

To improve your self-image, you need to experience being in that zone, where it's just you, your prowess, and the woman. Once you experience this, it will greatly boost your self-confidence and you will start to have a better view of yourself.

Experience is the key to unlocking this. Put yourself into more situations that challenge you. If it feels nerve racking, go for it. Travel as much as you can. Even better if you are alone because you will develop so much confidence through being in unfamiliar surroundings. Everyday try to grow a little bit. You see that hot girl walk past, approach her. There is a networking event on the weekend, go to it. Jump out of a plane? Do it!

However, keep in mind that there is a fine line between confidence and arrogance, and you do not want to confuse the two. Attractive males are not guys who strut around thinking they own the world and everyone else is beneath them. That's not how it is with them, which is why a lot of men look up to these guys. Unlike arrogant guys who end up having a lot of enemies because of their narcissistic attitude. Think about James Bond. He is the type of guy that attracts all the ladies but men admire them. When there is a problem, people go to him because they know that he can solve it. He is confident, not arrogant and people respect that.

Lose your ego

If you are controlled by your ego, then you cannot call yourself an alpha male because they know their limitations. They know that they are not gods who can do anything. Being controlled by your ego is a sign of weakness. You need to know how to bow down and be humble at the right time. Get out of your way and take responsibility for your actions, especially if you make a mistake. Saying sorry and admitting you are wrong is a sign of strength. This is where a lot of men fail. They think that admitting they are wrong will be the end of them when it is not. Living that way you will never grow and you will also alienate people from you.

Set Boundaries

Do not take bad behaviour from others. Do not be the nice guy all the time or you will end up being friend zoned by these ladies or worse, you will be treated as a doormat. Remember that the way people treat you reflects on the way you value yourself. If people take advantage of you, let them know or stop seeing them. You know your value and are strong enough to give but if there is no return, leave.

Love yourself first before you love others. Take my word for it because I have been there before. When I was still a student, girls would only come to me when they needed something, and I just let them because I didn't know any other way to attract girls. But when I finally decided that I'd had enough of that kind of treatment and stood up for myself, more girls wanted to talk to me. When you set your boundary and you don't take bad behaviour from others, they feel safe when they are with you. Women love that kind of power and confidence in a man.

While you are in the process of changing yourself, you will likely hear a lot of criticism from people around you because they are used to the old you. They accepted the loser, it's comfortable for them, but for you there is no progress there. Changing something about yourself, especially something major like changing your job or your personality is hard to swallow for most people around you. However, those people who matter, those who are your real friends, will stay with you and support you especially when they find out the reason behind the changes. They might be shocked at first and may even show signs of disapproval but at the end of the day, they will still be there for you. On the other hand, your so-called friends who cannot and do not want to try to understand what you are going through will permanently leave. And good riddance, if I may say so myself.

Forget What Others Think

They don't really matter. What's important is the outcome of all your efforts and the changes that you are making in your life. People will think you are weird for talking to girls you don't know. But it's more weird to stay at home fantasizing about them. Being out there will put you in the spotlight a little but what you will realize is that most people don't really see it or care. They are too caught up in their phones or day to day trivia to notice you.

Always remind yourself that improving yourself far exceeds the opinion of these people who don't really matter in your life. Just ignore them because you cannot please everybody. Life is a journey, not a destination and success relies on becoming better. We must all have goals but reaching them is not the real reward, the real power comes from what you have to do to get there.

Have Confidence in Yourself

Believe that you can get any girl that you want. This might come across as arrogance but this is just like a mantra that you can say to yourself every day when you wake up. You don't really need to shout this to the whole world so that everyone can hear. Just keep it to yourself as a daily reminder. This is especially useful when you are feeling low or in a high pressure environment. Not everyday will be a good day. There will be times when you feel like giving up but just continue with what you have started because you are the shit! Always psych yourself up when self-doubt starts to kick in because you do not want to drown in it.

Affirmations and asking questions of yourself are a great way to achieve this. Incorporate them as a part of your daily routine, perhaps when you take a shower you can say out loud your affirmations and ask questions. Some affirmations I have used and still use are:

I am confident

I am a winner

I am attractive and can seduce any woman I want

I look and feel awesome

I am charismatic and charming

These might seem highly arrogant or feel weird to say but it is sending confident messages to your subconscious mind that will have great results for your dating life. You can also bring out further good emotions such as asking. What am I grateful for? Why? How does it make me feel? Or, what am I happy about? Why? How does that make me feel? Take responsibility for the thoughts you put into your mind and exercise it regularly.

Meditation and cognitive therapy are also great activities to raise your confidence. Try sitting quietly with eyes closed or open for ten to twenty minutes at the start of everyday or the end as you prefer. Focus on deep breathes in and out. If a thought enters your mind, observe it. Instead of getting caught up in our emotions we can learn to distance ourselves and be in control or our mind. If you feel stressed, sad or depressed write down everything you feel. Read and add more. Unload your mind onto the pages. When you clear your mind and observe your thoughts it will give you more presence and clarity.

Man Up

How do you do this? No, I am not telling you to go out and pick fights with random strangers. That's not the definition of manning up. It means you need to face your fears. For instance, if you are afraid to go up to a girl and start a conversation with her, you need to overcome this fear if you want to be considered an alpha male. Don't be a pussy. Just think of her as another human being that you are talking to. Nothing too scary about that, right?

Another example of manning up is facing your responsibilities. If you got a girl pregnant, you need to man up and face your responsibility by supporting the child and not hiding your child from your prospective dates. Be a man and face the consequences of your actions.

My experience is also a good example of what not to do. When my first girlfriend was too busy with work, I whined and complained about it until she got fed up and broke up with me. Real men don't do this because they feel secure and they understand that their girlfriend's world does not revolve around them. They have their own purpose, life and hobbies. But now, when a girl tells me she is busy at work that's why she wasn't able to reply right away, I will simply say it's okay and no need to apologize, which is exactly what I feel. Don't be a whiney pussy who does not know what to do when his girl is not with him. Go out and get a life and you will see she will love you even more.

Know Your Value

Accept only the right kind of treatment from others. If you know your value, you will not allow people to treat you any less than you deserve. Always think that your value is at its maximum and it will not be touched or affected by outside factors. Just because you are trying to attract a woman does not mean you are willing to compromise your value. It should always be constant no matter what situation you are in. If you are rejected, do not think that your value becomes less. Just think of it as a learning experience that contributes to who you are as a person. Do not take it too seriously and just move on.

Finally, when it comes to wooing a woman, you will experience obstacles both great and small. Always **remind yourself that you can do anything** if you put your mind to it. Instead of shrinking away from the obstacles, find ways to remove them. For example, if a woman you like is currently in a relationship with someone, and you feel that she deserves better but she's just settling, you need to get rid of the obstacle—the boyfriend. Now don't take this literally. Don't go out searching for a hitman who can kill her boyfriend for you. Removing the obstacle means making the girl single again so that you can move in for the kill. You do not even really need to do anything. If you follow all the tips in this book and become the alpha male that all men want to be, just introducing yourself, talking to her, and letting her know that you are interested and just waiting on the sides until when they break up will be enough. No need to badmouth the guy or do anything underhanded. You might say that targeting a woman who is in a relationship is not something you feel comfortable doing but remember that dating is all but a game, and everyone is fair game. Don't worry too much about it because that's how life works.

Other obstacles that you might encounter is not having a lot of money for dating. The solution is to look for ways to earn more money or to find a better paying job. Always try to improve your situation.

You might also experience not having enough time to go out because of work. You can always try online dating or download dating apps such as Tinder. Every problem has a solution, sometimes solution is more than one. Become self aware and constantly review your progress so that you can identify challenges. Shrink these obstacles to a size that you can manage until they are completely gone.

You are now well prepared to search for these ladies now that you have improved your inner game. Women might be everywhere but there are great places to meet them. Find out more in the next chapters.

Chapter 4: How To Easily Meet Women

Finally, what you are all waiting for—meeting the women that we have been talking about since page one. Women are everywhere and as master seducers we need to consider the whole world around us.Life is a game. All day, all night you should be prepared to meet ladies. Maybe you are walking the dog, getting a haircut or at the airport. You see that hot girl and without excuses you approach her. How can you always do this consistently? The best advice I can give you for this is to develop your skills and personality. There are two ways to do this.

First, if you are a beginner or someone making a comeback then maybe you have a lot of anxiety about approaching women. Overcome this by immersing yourself into a period of constantly approaching women. Go out everyday and interact with women. Talk to the people in the shop, people who serve you food. Literally anyone you come across. Do not seek approval, the only win you gain is by opening your mouth and speaking. Their reaction is not important. In time you will gain more confidence in talking to strangers.

Second, talk with people as much as you can and incorporate it into your daily life. If you are served food or have to deal with people such as neighbours or service people then be friendly. Smile, try to make them laugh. Ask them how their day is going.

These points will prepare you and give you a natural reflex so that when you see that hot girl walk past you won't hesitate. Feeling good about yourself with also massively help you.

Smile, be confident and laugh at life.

Other places you can go to meet even more women include, classes, events, places of worship, fairs and much more.

Let's now look at some of the best places to meet women.

Chapter 5: Night Game

As I have said before, women are everywhere, and there are really good places to meet them. Just because there are women in your office does not mean you can flirt with only them. It has been done before and people fall in love with their coworkers all the time but it is something that you might want to avoid. You do not want to have your dating life and work life overlap especially when one of them goes sour. Just imagine the drama that you will have at work. There is an abundance of good single women out there in many places.

So where are the best places to meet women? And what kind of strategy do you need to use in certain situations? Check out the following tips and tricks.

I think that meeting women at night is easier than meeting them in the morning. This is because the darkness lends an air of romance, mystery, and also sexuality. People are more willing to let down their guard and be comfortable when it is night time than in broad daylight. Maybe because night is associated with relaxation, sleeping, and having sex, and it also marks the end of a whole day of working. Everyone who is still out at night is there to have a great time which means they are more open to meeting new people. This is my favorite game because I find it the easiest. And besides, I work best in the dark.

Where are the best places to practice your night game?

The most popular answer is the bar or club. Most women who go here want to meet new people and have a good time. Aside from the bar or club, you can also go to parties or events that are being held at night. Evening events and venues usually have booze, which makes it a lot easier to talk to people.

You can stay upto date with the latest and best events in your city by growing your social circle and also checking local events pages, meetup.com and facebook.

For beginners or those looking to elevate their skill, it is important to go out often, about four to five times per week. You might think it is too much especially if you have work during regular office hours but as they always say, no pain no gain, no guts no glory. Otherwise, how are you going to meet women if you rarely go out? On some nights this could be just an hour, the more your out there the more you gain confidence and get to meet more women.

You do not need to be with a group of friends. If you have no other option but to go by yourself, then by all means go out alone. It is, in fact, even better to go out alone especially once you get used to it because you can make your move without worrying about what your friends will think or without worrying about her falling for one of you friends instead of you. Working on your own is a lot better because you can focus on the task at hand. It will force you to talk to more people also. On the nights you go out with friends it's great for them to help you taking care of your girls friends so you can isolate her. Finding friends to go out with is easy, you can meet them out and about or on local forums, websites and social media.

To make sure you get a variety of experience, avoid going to the same place every night that you are out because you will probably see the same faces again and again. What I suggest is to list down all the places that you can go to for each day of the week that you are planning to go out. This makes it easier to work out a plan for the whole week. Thinking of where to go every time you want to go out can be draining, like always thinking of what to eat for dinner every day. So better do your research at the beginning of the week and create a schedule. That way when it comes to going out you have less excuses.

Before you go out, you need to prepare yourself with some pre go out preparation that will put you in the mood and in the right frame of mind.

Pre go out tips:

1. **Get in the right state**.
   To be in the right state for night game seduction, you need to be in the right frame of mind. You have to give yourself affirmations to psych yourself up. Tell yourself, "i am attractive and charming" or "I can do it!" or something along those lines. By voicing out positive statements, you are giving yourself positive vibes that can help you succeed in seducing women. Positive attracts positive. You can also ask questions as suggested in the previous chapter.

2. **Do some physiology at home**.
   What does this mean? It is not enough that you feed your mind positive thoughts to boost your confidence. You should also make your body more relaxed. I always do some light exercise for about 20 minutes if I still have time before I go out at night. I just do some stretching that helps release the tension in my muscles. If you are nervous because this is your first time and you are going out alone, just do some deep breaths to calm your nerves. If your body is relaxed, you will be more confident interacting with women that you will meet later. You can also put on some of your favourite songs and dance to them. This will put you in a great mood for sure.

3. **Warm up your voice**.
   This is especially true if you live alone and you have not spoken for hours. When you open your mouth to speak for the first time in hours, you might sound all squeaky, which can be a turn off for most girls. A common failure

when talking to girls at night is not even being heard by them. Most guys might think the girl doesn't like them, but really she can't hear you. Have a deep, strong, alpha voice. Practice your seduction voice before going out. If you have pickup lines, practice them using this voice and warm up your vocal chords.

4. **Look at yourself in the mirror**.
   This is not only for checking if you look good enough to sweep girls off their feet but also to practice different facial expressions such as smiling, smirking, squinting, winking, and so on. You might think you look seductive when you do that signature half-smile half-smirk of yours but you will not really know for sure unless you see it with your own two eyes. Try laughing at yourself for one whole minute. This will put you in a carefree happy state. Laughter is a powerful seduction tool.

5. **Be fun!**

   If you look too serious, nervous, or quiet when you go out, you will not meet any woman at all because they do not want to deal with guys like this. After all, they are there to have fun, remember? Just exude an aura of fun and keep pumping positive emotions. Stop being needy and seeking validation from others. Raise the level of the environment or match it.

You are now ready to go out! Remember that the night game begins right when you step out of your house. This is because you might just meet someone who just happens to walk by outside your place so be prepared the minute you go out. Even on the way you should be getting in the zone, talk with the taxi driver, make observations. When you arrive at the venue, you need to keep in mind several helpful tips and strategies that will make turn your night game into a successful one.

Exude a Sexual Vibe

Be a man that oozes sexuality. When you talk to a woman, she should immediately feel the sexual tension. To do this, you should learn how to talk seductively. Talk languidly, as if you have all the time in the world. Pause at the right moment to build intrigue. This is like dangling a piece of apple in front of a horse. The horse will want the apple even more. Flirt with the woman and maintain sexual eye contact. Have a powerful leading frame.

Smile

Smiling at people makes you look more approachable. Going back to the tip above, you should exude an aura of fun so that you will attract people. Women would not want to talk to you if you look annoyed, serious, or sad. You should always make it a point to look amused and friendly all the time. However don't be a clown, know when to use it and when to not.

Know the Venue's Rhythm

If this is your first time to go to that venue, you should first figure out the rhythm of the place before you make your move. For example, if a club opens at 8PM and closes at 3AM, this means that most women will be ready to leave by 12AM. Of course they would want to show off their outfits and their makeup in all their glory because they worked hard for it. Let them enjoy it before you decide to isolate them and pull them out of the club.

Social Proof

Social proof is an incredible tool that will help you pick up girls successfully. Honestly speaking, it is a kind of subtle mental manipulation that leads to your desired reaction from the ladies. It can be compared to advertising of a product. Even if you have no idea about a certain product, you still buy it based on the advertisements that you see.

To make it clearer, let's say you suddenly wake up in an unfamiliar place where you do not know anyone. You feel really hungry and you go out to eat. You see two unfamiliar restaurants. Restaurant A is full of people eating and talking. It looks like a happening place. Restaurant B looks empty, although the sign says they are open. Which restaurant would you choose if you are after delicious food? You will surely pick Restaurant A, because it has social proof. Unless of course you want to be alone and do not care too much about the food. Even if you have no idea about both restaurants, you judge them based on what you are seeing.

Another example is when you see someone wearing expensive clothes or driving an expensive car or eating at an expensive restaurant. You will automatically assume that the person is loaded even if you do not know him or her personally. It is what your eyes are seeing and based on that, your mind makes assumptions.

This is how social proof works. It is a psychological phenomenon wherein people look at what others are doing to make decisions in unfamiliar situations. Social proof is most obvious in unfamiliar situations, where people just look at others for guidance.

You can use this to your advantage when picking up girls. But how, you are probably asking? I'm sure you have been dying to know more about social proof and how it can help you get any girl you want.

There are three ways to use social proof when picking up girls:

1. Let women see you with other women/men
2. Be a social butterfly
3. Build in a place where you are known

The first point is to **let her see you with a group of people**. There are different kinds of groups that you may want her to see you with: a group of attractive women, a group of attractive men, a single attractive woman, and cool-looking buddy, or with a group of male and female friends. I put emphasis on the appearance of the people in your group because it plays a major role in social proof. When women see you with attractive people, they will automatically think you are also attractive because why else would these people swarm around you? You must have something special about you. So when you see your guy friends, use big gestures that everyone can see—high fives, man hugs, fist bump, etc. If you are out alone, work the crowd and let women see you interacting. Most guys think this might make them look a player, on the contrary as long as you are not making out with them or being overtly sexual then it will look as though these people are engaged by you. This is highly attractive behaviour.

Moreover, women judge you based on the people you are with. As the saying goes, birds of the same feather flock together. So if you are with your middle-aged buddies with beer bellies and receding hairline, you might get low points from the ladies. But if you are with young foxes wearing stylish clothes and looking all dapper, then the ladies will surely give you a high score in their book. Don't be afraid to approach high value people like this, try and find out. Often times they will be friendly.

Of course, it is important that these people in your group are doting on you. Or at least let women see that you and your group are having a great time. Women instantly notice the guy who commands attention. he is surrounded by people and they listen to him with rapt attention. I have seen lady friends before ask about a guy because they see him talking to a group of people and these people are looking up to him. Ladies just find these guys interesting to know.

Furthermore, social proof places a higher importance towards having fans than friends. This only applies to the dating game, not the real world, so don't go discarding your friends just because you need fans more. The reason why fans are more important than friends is because it only shows that you are at the top level of the social hierarchy, which makes you even more desirable among women.

You might ask, how can you acquire fans? You're not exactly a celebrity. Well, you can be one. At least at the bar where you frequent. You can either bring a group of young women or men with you, or you can go around the bar and talk to people, which brings me to the second point of social proof—**be a social butterfly.**

Talk to anyone you meet. And when I say anyone, I mean ANYONE—fat girls, shy girls, dudes, etc. Do not discriminate who you are friendly to because the ladies will notice this. Besides, the more people you talk to, the more popular you become. Even if they are considered lower in value when it comes to the hierarchy of dating, you should still go talk to them. First off, try to achieve the tasks that are easiest to achieve, or the low hanging fruits. Consider this as your warm up before you face the ultimate challenge.

If you do this, it will make you stand out when you finally approach the hottie because everyone already knows you. This will also increase your value in the eyes of the people around you. Just have a good time and enjoy the place and the people you meet. No pressure for now. Do not be too harsh on yourself at this stage because you are just starting. Any action taken is a positive.

However, one word of advice if you do decide to take this path—do not fall into entertainer mode, or high energy, or you would end up being the 'joker' or 'class clown' instead of the seducer. What you can do is to find the right balance between the two. Be Mr. Energetic while working your way around the room, and switch to seducer mode by lowering your energy when you finally found your target.

The trick here is to keep moving until you find the girl you like. After all, you do not want to spend all your time and energy and get stuck talking to someone you are not really interested in. And of course, you need to stop moving once you find the girl that you really like. This is one danger of becoming a social butterfly. You tend to build so much momentum talking to everyone that when you finally come across someone you really like, you still continue talking to other people because you find it difficult to decrease the momentum. Just do not lose focus on your goal. Remember that you are not here to entertain people, but to find a girlfriend, or at least someone to go home with for the night.

And finally, the third point, you need to **build your game in a place where you are known.** Of course, the first thing that you need to do is to be known in that place. It shouldn't just be any place. You need to know more about the venue before you start building your game. A great place for building your game is somewhere that has a lot of female patrons because how are you going to meet women if there are only a few of them? It should also be a place where people meet instead of doing other things such as dancing or eating with friends. It is also a plus if the place has areas where you can talk (or make out) to the lady in private. The club where I sometimes DJ has multiple floors. This gives people plenty of places to meet and talk. It is like having a venue within a venue.

After identifying the place where you want to be known, you can now start introducing yourself to the staff or even the owner. Talk to the bartender or wait staff. Have a word with the manager or owner. Go there not only when the place is hopping, but also during off days or a few hours before opening so that you can talk to the staff when they are not busy.

Once you get to know the people who work there, you will learn a lot of useful information about the people who usually go there. Moreover, when women see that you are friendly with the owner, manager, or staff, they will think you are somebody important, or that you have the right connections. This is also beneficial because building your game in a place where you are known and you feel comfortable will make things easier for you.

Social proof is highly effective in a place where there are a lot of potential women to meet but low receptivity. And if you do decide to apply social proof in your night game, you need to remember to take action right away. In the dating game, talk is cheap. Although verbal communication is important, nonverbal communication is even more important in dating because more often than not, it says a lot more than words ever will, which leads us to another strategy that you can employ in the night game—kino escalation.

Night Game Summary

These strategies are so effective that I still use them up to this day. After using them several times, they will come out naturally whenever you go out and want to pick up ladies.

So basically, here is how a night game will look:

In every step of the way you should always ask yourself **"what do I want?"**

Identifying your goals is important to keep your focus.

You need to apply this system with every girl that you meet. Consider it as a cycle. One girl is one cycle. Once you finish one cycle, you have to start all over again.

Move

Go around and introduce yourself to people. Meet new people.

- Go to the dance floor and dance for a bit.
- Loosen up, laugh feel the music, let loose and enjoy the venue.
- Talk with anyone to get into the zone

Open

Look for IOIs or indicators of interest (eye contact, small smile, hair flip, etc.) When you see this, send her back a signal like a wink, nod, gesture or smile. Go to the girl and say something like "hey, you know what this music reminds me of?" or use humor. Use physical contact early on such as shaking her hand because the longer you don't do initiate physical contact, the weirder it gets once you finally decide to do it.

Demonstrate Higher Value

You do not really need to brag about yourself. You can do it in a subtle way. I am a DJ and I sometimes tell stories about my work, like celebrities I met or events I DJ'd in. People ask, so I just answer. But I never go around telling people that I know this celebrity or I have been to this famous event unless someone asks. This will make you seem really cool and confident.

Vibe

Lead with the girl by talking to her, or dancing with her. Find out her logistics at the beginning of the set—if she lives alone, if she's with her friends, what her plans are tomorrow. This is the perfect time to make plans with her.

- Ask yourself "how can I make this fun? "Think of pickup openers that will get her to talk to you.
- Use FTC or false time constraint, tell her "I need to go back to my friends but before I do, can you please tell me..."
- Let the girl know that you find her attractive.

Let's say you finally found the girl that you like. Here is what should happen while you are in set, meaning while you are talking to the girl.

In Set

Vibe with her by building comfort and using humor. Assume things about the girl by starting your sentences with "I bet you are...", "you look like someone who...", "I think you are...". This creates attraction especially if your guesses are correct and elevates your status in the eyes of the lady.

Practice the push/pull method. Give her compliments and also negs. Negs or negatives are not insults. These are used to lower down the bitch shield of the ladies, and are extremely useful when interacting with a highly attractive females. These females are so used to men hitting on them that showering them with compliments will only make them uninterested. Instead, push them away a little bit by saying negs, such as "We probably won't get along because we're too much alike! "Or "I didn't know you are just as terrible as I am when it comes to dancing!" This will make her more comfortable enough to lower her bitch shield because she knows that you are not hitting on her.

Do not supplicate, or agree with everything she says, or be extremely amiable. Do not do or say things just for the sake of gaining her approval. Women see this as a sign of weakness. Keep the tension while you are in set. Keep her guessing but also sprinkle some SOIs or show of interest such as giving her a sincere compliment or using positive body language.

Give her plenty of space during the conversation. This means that you should not do the talking all the time. Don't make it look like an interview where you ask questions and she responds. She should also do her part by asking questions to you in return. If there is a lull in the conversation, let her fill in the silence especially after doing your part. The most powerful social force is space.

Get her invested. If the girl is invested, she will be more willing to go further. One way to do this is to get her invested emotionally. Yes, you can do this even during the initial meet. You should say something personal about yourself first, then ask her if she has experienced the same thing. Once she opens up to you, she is already investing emotionally. If she buys you a drink or pays for your food, she is investing financially. Investing is a huge IOI because only people who are interested will take the time and effort to do such things.

Paint pictures and sounds while talking to the girl. This will make her more interested to get to know you better, which could lead to making out, then sex.

While Still in Set

Talk with emotion. Do not be like an interviewer who only asks questions and do not show any kind of emotion while talking. Turn the conversation to something deeper and more serious. Ask her questions such as "what is your biggest fear?" or "if you could choose to live anywhere, where would you live? "Questions like these require an elaborate answer that gives you a glimpse of the person.

As I have said before, use emotional spikes. Make her feel different kinds of emotions while talking to you. Make it feel like a roller coaster ride for her. Use push and pull. Push her away and pull her back in. Do not be scared to use this on women because they are pros at this kind of thing. They let you wonder whether she is really interested or not. Why not do the same thing to her? Let her wonder. By doing the push-pull technique, it's like you are telling the woman, "I really like you... I think. We should probably date...or not."

Make her qualify by letting her talk a bit about herself. You will know if she is someone you would like to date if she starts to tell you things about herself. And always give her plenty of space to contribute to the conversation. Don't do all the work.

Social Dynamics

Often times she may be with a group of friends. You can use the people you are with to your advantage. Use your friends to help you get to her. Or if you have girl friends, you can ask them to introduce you to their girl friends, remember that girls are better connected than men and they will surely have someone for you if you cannot find one for yourself.

If she has friends with her, get her to introduce you to her friends. This is important because if she introduces you to her friends, it simply means she likes you. And when she does, be sure to game the whole group. She will know that you are valuable when she sees her friends enjoying talking to you. It will definitely increase your desirability. Who knows, maybe you will find someone you like more among her friends, although it is something I advise against doing when you already started showing your interest and making your move to one particular girl because you do not want to cause animosity among them. Always make sure her friends like you and trust you, when it comes to going home they will often encourage her to go with you.

Lead and Seed the Pull

Always have a winning mindset. During your interaction make sure you find out her logistics. Find a place in the venue where you can isolate her. Or better yet, figure out a way to bring her home or to make her invite you to her home.

Who is she here with?

Where is she going next?

What is she doing the next day?

These key questions will tell you how likely the pull is. If your looking for a simple one night stand then move on fi her answers make the situation seem too difficult. If the logistics are good then start seeding the pull. Suggest drinks at your place after, tell her about where you live. Plant the seed in her mind and gauge the reaction.

Pull

After seeding the pull, you can now finally close the set, by changing the location. You can either go somewhere private in the venue or find an excuse to go home with her. Tell her your having an after party, or come check out my new music collection. Any semi valid reason will do. Just keep her logical mind distracted by talking to her. Do not allow her to have second thoughts even for a minute because this can make her change her mind.

Let's assume that you have pulled her to your home, her home or hotel (or bathroom ;)

Although bringing her to your house means you want to have sex with her, you have to still make it fun and interesting for her. Show her around your house, play some relaxing music, prepare food and drinks, just basically be a good host. Don't just enter the door and start having sex with her because that's just not how it should be done. Unless both of you are extremely in heat and want to do away with the niceties.

Gradually start to make things more sexual. Use physical kino escalation (see the chapter on sex for more information). Usually, it starts from eye to body. Meaning you are checking out the girl. Then eye to eye. Or both of you looking at each other. The first physical contact usually starts when you touch her hand, arm, or elbow. You are not suggesting anything yet but merely testing the waters. If her reaction is positive, you can start putting your arms around her shoulders or on her waist and lower back. Stroke her knees, if you will. This should be done smoothly. You shouldn't just put your hands on her waist out of nowhere. You can do this when you are leading her to the door or dance floor. Once all these innocent gestures are done, which you have probably done already while still in the club, you can now proceed to more sexual actions, like kissing and groping.

There are telltale signs that she is ready to be kissed, or in fact, practically asking you to kiss her. Her intense gaze and slightly open mouth are indications that she is ready to go further. You will also notice her chest is slightly arched, as if inviting you to come closer. Put your arms around her and go in for the kiss.

Once you are kissing, groping automatically comes next. Put your hands under her shirt, just to touch her stomach. If she doesn't resist, touch her more private parts, like her breasts and genitals. Make sure you do this in a private location! Because this will ultimately lead to sex. Do not forget to compliment her body, because this will turn her on even more. Oh and always use protection. You don't want any surpises!

Wow! We're done tackling night game seduction. It is more detailed and comprehensive because picking up women is usually done at night because it is more effective. However, this does not mean that you can't do it in during the day. That's why we also need to learn day game techniques.

Chapter 6: Day Game

If there is something called night game in the art of seduction, there is surely something called day game. Obviously, this is done during the day, which a lot of men think is not a good time to pick up girls. They are wrong, of course, because anytime is a good time to pick up girls as long as you know what you are doing.

So imagine yourself jogging in the morning, just like you normally do. Then you suddenly see a really attractive girl going in the opposite direction. What do you do? You cannot just simply stop her and talk to her without an action plan in mind. Although, of course, you can do this but it's not ideal. She might find you weird, or worse, dangerous, if you don't do it the right way.

The "game" is not just done in bars, clubs, parties, or any other social gatherings at night. It can be practically anywhere—in parks, classes, café, malls, libraries, shops, on train platforms, galleries, or even your usual jogging route. You can find girls anywhere, therefore, you can pick up girls anywhere.

The main difference between a night game and a day game is that night game venues are specifically designed for people to mingle or interact with each other, while day game venues are not specifically designed for this purpose.

People who are out and about during the day are usually busy because they have somewhere to go to or are running errands. People who go out at night are out because they want to meet new people or just want to have a good time. So which game is easier and which one is more difficult for pickup artists? Night game is easier, and day game is more difficult. But of course, you still have to do it because it is still a great opportunity to meet women.

Here are the things that you need to do when picking up women during the day.

Opening

The most difficult part of the day game is opening. How are you going to approach the hot girl in broad daylight without looking like a creepy stalker? The secret is to do it as spontaneously and naturally as possible, as if you have just seen her that exact moment that you are talking to her, and not sometime ago when you started following her every move. The quicker you approach the more spontaneous and natural it will be. Just make sure you have observed your surroundings first. Is she with her boyfriend? Is she with her family or friends? Is she in a rush?

To approach the woman, you have to put a friendly smile on your face. Make it look like you are fun and friendly to talk to. If you have never done it before it might seem very intimidating, try to overcome this by first asking strangers for the time or directions. It might seem silly but will put you in the right frame of mind.

Talk clearly. The first words that you may want to utter to someone who is going about her day and minding her own business is "excuse me?" because you don't want to scare her by introducing yourself right away and telling her that she's cute.

Just like in the night game, you should also use FTC or false time constraints in the day game. Say something like, "I'm on my way to my friend's house but I can't help but notice..." or "I have to go catch the train in a few minutes but I just saw you and wanted to say..."

As an opening, you can give her a compliment, state an observation about your surroundings, ask for her opinion, and so on. Just be sure that it is something unique and original, something she hasn't heard of before. This will make you stand out among all the guys who tried to pick her up.

If she looks like she is doing something or is in a hurry, you can be direct in approaching her. At least she won't think that you are ruining her schedule, which will only make her not only uninterested but also annoyed. If she finds you interesting, your FTC will be a lot more advantageous because she will think she might lose you any minutes, and she might find a way to have a contact with you before you leave, such as giving you her number.

Maybe she is with friends or even family. Don't be put off by that, most girls won't be alone. If you find her attractive just go up and be really polite and introduce yourself. The people with her will be impressed by that and so will she for the confidence you showed.

And one word of advice from an expert, when she already sees you, do not hesitate because women can sense your hesitation a mile away and this is a huge turnoff for them. And your game is already ruined because her initial impression of you is already awkward and unconfident. Never hide because it's just plain creepy, dude. When you talk to her, be confident and talk audibly.

The Conversation

Basically, a huge chunk of the day game is the conversation itself. Assuming that she is not in any hurry, you can have a conversation with her. Find a topic of conversation that both of you can relate to. You don't really know anything about the girl yet, so the safest topics are anything related to your present situation. For example, if you are at a store and the lines at the cash register are pretty long, you can say something about it, then ask her about her purchases, if she always shops there, etc. Or if you are both attending a cooking class, you can talk about the class itself, such as the parts that you like and you don't like, what makes you decide to take a cooking class, and so on.

Your first conversation is not the time to get deeper and know more about the girl. You are just in the process of introducing yourself to each other and of course, securing her number and possibly a second meetup or a date. Do not ask her stuff out of nowhere, such as what her favorite color is or anything too personal, like her past relationships, unless the conversation went in that direction naturally. Do not force the flow of the conversation but rather make it go as smoothly and naturally as possible.

Before ending the conversation, or your first meeting, be sure to get her number or arrange a second meeting or a date. Say something along the lines of "Listen, I really want to know more about that museum you were telling me about. Can we visit it tomorrow, if you have free time? "Or "I really think you can help me with this topic, can we meet up later and talk about it more?" And if you can't think of something creative, just be straightforward: "I really enjoyed talking to you and would like to continue this conversation. Are you free later for dinner?"

You can also go on a date with her right away. This is great if she is available now because you can get to know eachother, build rapport and save time. In some cases you can even close the deal on the same day. I have often done this, you better believe it is possible! To do this just ask her if she wants to get a drink and chat for a few minutes. You can use the false time constraint again. On you date you can test the water, find out her logistics, move the conversation to various topics. Talk about sex, find out her level of comfort and how ready she is. If she seems really turned on change venue or suggest going somewhere more private. You can also use kino escalation the whole time. For example, check out her jewelry, test her muscles or hold her hands.

Day game can be practiced anytime, anywhere. For beginners, try approaching women that you are not really interested in dating in a nice, friendly manner. Ask them about their day, what they are doing there, etc. You will often face rejection or embarrassing situations but push forward because the positive outweigh the negative. Remain cheerful, polite and friendly. As a beginner you can take it step by step. Try going out of your house for an hour a day and just ask people for directions. Push the conversation more each time. Incorporate approaching into your daily life so when you see the hot girl walk past you on your way to grocery shopping you can approach her with ease. You do not really need to get their number or ask them out on a date. You can just end the conversation by simply saying, "It was nice talking to you. Have a great day!" When you develop your confidence you can move towards more advanced levels.

Day game is a great way to meet different types of women. You often won't meet them in clubs or online. They are often good girls with stable lifes. Some of the best women I have personally met are through day game. The opportunity is huge because hardly any guy has the balls to do it. Girls will find it highly romantic if you pull it off. Because for her it's like a movie scene, I met this guy in the coffee shop or on the train, etc.

The majority of day game is played slower and does not really lead to hooking up or sex right away. Although as I have said, that can happen! The ultimate goal of picking up girls during broad daylight is simply getting her number and securing dates either later on the same day or in the near future.

When you have their numbers put them into your phone and schedule plans with them. Set goals and move forward.

Chapter 7: Online Dating

In this modern age of technology, everything can be done online, even dating. Some people treat online dating as their last resort and often feel embarrassed talking about it. But that shouldn't be the case. A lot of people have found their lifelong partners online. Online dating has become so common that you shouldn't feel embarrassed about it anymore. A lot of people, old and young, are doing it. Some celebrities have even confessed to using it. In dating, you should exhaust all your possibilities because who knows, the one you are looking for might be too busy to go out and prefers online dating.

The thing with online dating is that there are so many guys who send dirty pictures and disrespectful messages that good guys, like you and me, sometimes don't stand a chance. We are lumped together with these guys who think sending pictures of their dick makes them attractive for some reason. Thankfully, this image of online dating is slowly beginning to change, when more and more people use it, unlike before when it's mostly used by unattractive people who have weird fetishes. Now, even popular people use it, especially with the popularity of Tinder. If you haven't heard of this, you must be living under a rock and you should definitely start brushing up on your dating knowledge.

If you belong to that handful of people who haven't tried Tinder before, it is an online app that you can download on your mobile phone. It doesn't have the hassle of creating a dating profile because it is connected to your Facebook account. The basic premise of Tinder is that if you like a picture, you swipe right. If you don't like it, you swipe left. If both of you swipe right on each other's picture, Tinder will create a match then you can start chatting. It may sound shallow because you are basically judging a person based on her looks (or profile picture) but isn't that how normal dating works as well? You approach a woman because of how she looks. Personality and other deeper stuff will come next. That's the same thing for online dating. You can both swipe right but for it to go any further depends on whether or not you clicked after having online conversations.

You can also subscribe to Tinder Plus, which features five Super Likes per day, one, rewind last swipe, unlimited likes, and passport to swipe around the world. This is a great feature if you are a traveling man because you can set up dates ready for when you land. If you use the paid version of Tinder you can use great features such as the Boost. When you use this, your profile will be placed at the top of the other profiles that your potential matches can see for 30 minutes, which means more chances of getting your profile swiped right.

There is also Tinder Gold, which is basically like Tinder Plus plus one more feature—it allows you to see who likes you. Tinder also has a feature called "Super Like" where it allows you to alert a potential Tinder match that you are super attracted to her before you swipe right. You can't explain it but there's something about the picture that gives you butterflies even before meeting them or talking to them. It happens sometimes, right?

Your profile on Tinder needs to be optimized. You can use upto six pictures of yourself with one as your main profile picture. There is also a feature which selects your best picture by using some algorithms. You can rely on that but it is best to select photos that display you has an attractive man. For example, travel photos, health/gym photos, photos with attractive women, photos with friends, high quality fashion photos (great for the profile picture), photos with animals and any other attractive photos of you. Avoid cliche pictures such as low quality selfies, shirtless pictures of general sleazy looking pictures. Pay a professional photographer to take some quality photos of you. Test various selections, ask your girl friends and find what works for you best. You can always delete your account and start again if it isn't working out. You will then have a second shot at the women!

Tinder also features a description/bio section. You might think this is not important because us guys are highly visual, but women often read this. Use this to describe yourself in a short, sweet, attractive and funny way that provokes a response. For example, can you bake cookies? What's a funny story you can tell me? Things like this will provoke the girl to contact you. Or you could say my ex threw a brick through my window, hope your not crazy or I am a famous DJ. These will make the girl curious and likely to contact you. List your hobbies and interests briefly. If your a tall guy list your height. It is not important if you of average height but for tall guys it is dynamite.

Just like with normal dating, you also need an opening chat message. Say something like "We both swiped right so I guess we're a perfect match." Or "Hello there, adorable Tinder match." Or "Did anyone tell you that you look like (a celebrity). That's why I swiped right." Or "I heard Chinese girls are…"Any opening statement that is witty or any compliment to start off the conversation on a positive note will do. There are also GIF's that you can use to start conversations in a funny way. Just be respectful.

Now that you have started the conversation, you can find similar interests or hobbies that will let you know if you have something in common. The thing with online dating is that it is easier to open a conversation because you have time to come up with a witty statement, plus asking about her likes and dislikes on the first day is not so weird.

You can also send pictures to each other (no dick pics, for god's sake) or voice messages. Tell her more details about yourself such as your height, hobbies, likes, work, and soon.

You can tell her your location (not your exact address) so that you will know if there is a chance for you to meet up.

If you like what you are seeing (or reading) so far, and if you think she is also interested you can then ask for her number or contact details for another app to talk on.

Switching to another app will get her more invested in you, its like a location change in real life. You are leading and she is following. A great app to use for this is Instagram. This will show her more about you and likewise for her. Make sure you have a great profile, post cool photos of you traveling, having a good time, with your friends and other attractive pictures. She will be more likely to meet you if she knows more about you.

When you have her contact you can get her more invested. Send funny pictures of what your doing, send voice messages and make her more familiar to you. Give her a call and get to know each other even more. Once you decided to meet up, set the date and place. It is best to choose a location that you think is safe, like your local gym, yoga class, park, restaurant, and so on.

And aside from Tinder, you can also use social media platforms to find hookups or dates, such as Facebook or Instagram.

On Facebook and Instagram add or follow, different hot girls and start talking with them. Like her pictures, send a DM or direct message, get her invested. If she doesn't respond, move on. These apps have great features you can use for dating such as stories and locations. Stories can be used to test how into you the girl really is. Is she watching you? It is also great for starting conversations. Locations can be used to find out where all the hot girls are!

With these apps, don't just focus on one girl. Add or follow as many girls as you like on Facebook or Instagram. Again, make sure your profile is looking great.

Just remember that no matter what online dating platform you use, you should always be respectful so that you won't be lumped together with those other guys who think their dicks are God's gifts to girls. Be interesting, funny and listen to her.

Chapter 8: Get Girls at Work

Did you know that there are jobs out there that are designed for you to get laid? Well, not exactly "designed "for that purpose but you get my drift. If you work in an office setting, it might be more difficult to get laid because of the environment. The mail room or pantry is not exactly a great place for romantic encounters. I know you are probably thinking that you have seen a lot of movies or tv shows that have coworkers fall in love with each other and have sex in the office. Sure, this can be done but it is still not the ideal place.

And besides, going out every night to meet girls can be exhausting, not to mention expensive. So the solution is to find a job that can get you laid. It's a win-win situation for you. You are earning money while effortlessly picking up girls at the same time.

I am a DJ and I can vouch for this job. I meet so many women in a week that choosing is a must because there's not enough time to date them all. I am always surrounded by women, fighting for my attention. Women will often approach me and give me their numbers. And all I have to do is play music. It's so easy it's laughable.

Aside from DJs, bartenders also get a lot of dates. However, the job of a bartender is more difficult than a DJ. What I would recommend is to be a bartender in high end hotel bars that do not have drunken idiots that make bartending difficult in some venues. Other jobs that give you more opportunities to get laid are masseuse, personal trainer, dance instructor, gym instructor, musician, tattoo artist, photographer, and stripper. If you still want a job that is still kind of corporate but allows you to meet new people, you can try sales. This will also develop your confidence talking to strangers.

Remember to apply the principles you have previously learned when talking to women at work. Be sure that you come off as an attractive and confident man. Don't be creepy.

Many of these jobs you can take on part time and it will give you the chance to still keep your main job or studies. You can always go through a period of deep immersion into meeting as many women as possible. Whether that be through, night, day, online, social circle or job. Your whole life should be viewed as an opportunity to meet women. Never miss an opportunity.

Chapter 9: Social Circle

Social Circles are an easy and convenient way to hook up with lots of women. Some nights you won't want to be at the club. Day game can be hard to do all the time and online game can lead to a lot of flakes. Having a great social circle fills the gaps and brings you a constant stream of new girls.

Social circle is all about making friends with a lot of different people who are popular and always out and about. For example I know people working in PR whose job it is to know lots of hot girls. These guys or girls are always with lots of people and you should make an effort to befriend them. If you see a guy in a club surrounded by hot girls. Make friends with him. Don't be the guy who tries to steal his girls. Think long term and become part of his network so you too can have an endless supply of girls. Add value to them.

People working for model talent agencies are also great to know because models often are on short term contracts so they have a new supply coming into town always. These people are responsible for bringing them to the best parties. If you are friends with them then you will be already a cool guy in their eyes because you have social proof and pre selection of the group.

Other people with large social circles include, DJ's, artists, business owners and successful charismatic people. You should always be focused on meeting new people and making friends with them. Ask to be introduced, approach cool people and embrace the unknown. You can even go to local meetups and events to bring you into contact with more people. The power is in the people you know.

Can men and women be friends? Absolutely, not every girl you talk to you will sleep with. Sometimes you friend zone them or she isn't into you that way. Or maybe you used to date. Females are great friends for men to add to their social circle. They will give you feedback from a woman's perspective and also lots of social proof to the girls you date.

Having a big social circle will do wonders for your life, you will get invited to exclusive parties, go on amazing trips and be introduced to cute girls who are friends with your friends. It will also allow you to always have people to go out with.

Keep a track of all your contacts and maintain your network. Make sure that you add value to them always. Send a nice text here and there will be a great gesture. Invite them out, have a conversation, share cool things. Facebook and Instagram are great apps to keep upto date with your friends, their life and the events they attend.

Chapter 10: Follow Up and Keep Women Interested

When you first meet a woman or talk online it's a good idea to get her contact details so that you can follow her up and keep her interested. Texting and calling occur when you have successfully acquired a girls number. There are certain rules that you need to follow for numbers to turn into dates and more.

When to send the first text? There is no right answer to this. Sometimes I have waited a week or more, sometimes instantly. It's not really that important, just be calibrated when you do it. Usually I send a text within the day of meeting her, you want to keep it fresh. If you sent a text right away it should be short and sweet. Nice to meet you will do. If it is much later on, something such as hey how was your week? Sorry have been quiet, life has been busy.

The main focus is to build comfort with her and to get her more invested so that she will meet you. Have a witty attitude that is fun and lifts her spirits. For instance, you should be witty but not too clever because that will make you sound like a know-it-all nerd. You do not want to turn her off by spouting unnecessary facts in your text messages or phone calls. Avoid being boring and logical. Be interesting and not like the other guys. Have funny answers to standard questions.

Where are you from? Just came from the supermarket

How old are you? 74 years old

Try not to be overly funny, just a little. Tease her and paint imaginary scenarios between the two of you. Give her a compliment to put her in a better mental space. "I really like your profile picture" or "I'd like to get to know you better because you seem like an interesting person." She's more likely to reply to your messages and phone calls.

Get her more invested. Send her voice messages, GIFs, videos, and pictures but remember not to bombard her by sending her a message or calling her every few minutes or hours. As I have mentioned before, space is an important tool in communicating. Give her plenty of space, let her miss you. If she doesn't reply in a few minutes, just wait. Do not send multiple texts or make several calls without her replying because you would look desperate. Or worse, a creepy stalker. Always reply less than she does. Investment should be more from her.

When you are texting you should also not ask too many questions. Save all these questions for later when you are talking to her in person. As a rule ask only one question per time. Keep in mind not to let the conversation go on too long, the goal is to move it towards a meeting as soon as possible.

If a girl doesn't text you back right away or ignores your calls don't take it too seriously or be one of those name calling abusive guys. Maybe she is busy, act cool at all times. If she takes too long, send a reminder. If she still doesn't reply then forget it and move on. Maybe she met someone else, who knows and who cares. You have abundance.

This is why it is important to talk to multiple girls at the same time, until you find the perfect one because you won't notice if one of them takes a long time to respond. Moreover, when she finally replies, do not send her a reply right away, as if you are looking at your phone waiting for her messages, as if you do not have anything better to do in life.

Having a phone call is a great way to build more comfort. One tip if you are going to make a phone call, you need to find an excuse why you are calling her because calling is a bigger investment than simply chatting or sending a text message. It is not only more expensive to call but it also shows that you are more invested in her emotionally. This is why you need to find an excuse for calling her. Tell her that your screen is broken and you cannot clearly see messages that's why you called.

The goal of texting and calling is to make her more comfortable about meeting up with you and also for you to find out if you want to pursue her. Maybe she is super annoying or boring and you can take the quick exit. If you like her build the comfort and investment to get her to meet with you for a date.

During your texting or calling you need to move the conversation towards a meeting. Ask her out on a date, by simply saying "Are you doing anything fun this week? Want to hang out?" or "What kind of music do you listen to? Because there's this one bar that just opened and would want to check it out. Want to come?"

You should have your week planned out with days available for dates and a choice of girls you want to meet. Your in control and your the alpha male.

Speaking of dates, you also need to know some useful tips and tricks about dating because it is not as simple as they make it out in the movies, especially if you are trying to get laid.

Chapter 11: How to Date High Quality Women

You are almost there. You have finally secured a date with the girl you like. When you are already out on a date with her, you need to know what to do. It is not as simple as meeting her somewhere and having a conversation. You need to do some techniques that will help you get laid on the first date. Or pursue a serious relationship with the girl.

First and foremost, the time and day. The perfect time for dates is 8PM. It's not too early that you both don't need to rush off from work, and it is also not too late which will only give you a short time to apply your seduction skills. The day should be convenient to you, make sure your schedule is clear so that you can close the date if you want to.

When choosing the place, you need to consider three things. Location, activity and vibe. Each depends on the level of investment the girl has in you and what type of girl she is. For good girls who are more conservative it's usually best to have a short sweet first date, maybe a hour for drinks at a chilled out bar or cafe. This will be great to show her your a decent guy and can be trusted. The next date you can escalate more. It is always to your advantage to close (have sex with) your dates as soon as possible. This will take out all of the games and neediness. It will also show you if you really like the girl.

Location

You should aim for places near to your home. This will make it easy to take her back with you. You don't want to get stranded far away from home. However for first time dates it's not too important because you are less likely to close the deal. On later dates you can bring them closer to your place.

Activity

Informal drinks are best for a first date because you can have conversations and kino easily. Avoid restaurants or cinemas for early dating because they will make it hard to talk or escalate physically. Other great activities include, a walk in the park, shopping, exercise or classes.

Vibe

The first dates should have a vibe where it is more intimate. You don't want the distraction of other people such as in clubs or noisy bars. Choosing places where you are known are great because it raises your social proof.

If you have multiple dates in a week, you might want to do the same routine with all of them because it makes things easier for you. Just be careful that there are not any jealous people around who might tell the girl you were there last night with someone else.

When you are already on a date with her, do not lose the momentum. You have to act quickly or the moment for seduction or sex will be gone. This is why it is important to take the initiative in all areas—texting, setting up dates, inviting her home, etc.—because it gives you the right momentum that you need. Strike while the iron is hot, so to speak. But of course, you should still not act all needy and desperate. You already did your part by taking the initiative. Let her do hers by responding to not only to your messages but also to your advances.

The thing with going out on a date unprepared is that you are just relying on your own communication skills and the ambience of the place. Of course these are important but you also need to have a technique that will ensure you are going to get laid later. You need to be the kind of man who can press the right buttons and make any girl fall madly in love with you.

How do you make a girl fall head over heels in love with you after just meeting her for the first, or even second time? The trick here is to make her feel comfortable with you. Sex does not just stem from attraction. Being comfortable with the person is also a main ingredient. Many dating experts believe that the formula for sex is 30% attraction and 70% comfort. Attraction is important because if there is only comfort, you will end up being friendzoned by the girl. On the other hand, if there is only attraction, it will not lead anywhere. It will just be like crushing on somebody, like a celebrity, because you do not feel comfortable enough to make it go any further.

So, you already know that she is attracted because she said 'yes' when you asked her out on a date. How do you make her feel comfortable? The answer is the "Boyfriend-Her" technique.

Basically, it is doing things that only a long-time boyfriend would normally do. Women trust their boyfriends and they feel comfortable with them. How do you act like her boyfriend even if you are not really her boyfriend? When you see a couple together, you will notice that they do not just touch each other romantically. They also do things that only people comfortable with each other will do, such as removing crusties from each other's eyes. It might be gross for some people but definitely not when you are doing it with someone you love.

Now, don't start looking for crusties in her eyes just to make her feel comfortable with you. It can be something simple as brushing her hair behind her ears, removing dirt off her clothes, tying her shoelaces, and so on. Boyfriends do these to their girlfriends. And this makes girls feel comfortable. You can act like her boyfriend in this manner and make her feel comfortable as well. If she is comfortable enough, you will surely end up getting laid if you play your cards right.

Make sure you have a great plan to change locations from your first meeting to your place. And how can you make a girl come home with you? Find an excuse to do it. Of course, most girls already know that you are attracted to her and would like to sleep with her but in the kind of society we live in, you don't exactly say these things directly. You just imply it. Just find an excuse to invite her to your home. "Would you like to have a drink or two in my apartment?" "I'd like to show you my studio." "I need to go pick up my washing." Anything just to make her come home with you without expressly saying you want to take her home to have sex with her.

And your home should be a good place for seduction. Before going out, hide anything that can ruin the mood, such as your pile of unwashed laundry or empty beer cans. The place should look like an elegant bachelor's pad. And the venue of your date should just be near your place so that you can take her home with you anytime.

When you are already home, set the mood by putting on some relaxing music and not turning on all the lights. Prepare drinks for both of you and show her some normal stuff just to make her feel at home. Use kino escalation, together with the "Boyfriend-Her" technique, and you would have her in your bed in no time. Other things that you might want to try is massage or lighting up candles.

The truth is, you can get laid anytime, anywhere. You can get laid at night, during the day, at the gym, in a class, etc. But of course, the perfect time is at night and somewhere private where you can do anything you want, like your place.

Basically, here is how the entire dating scenario should look like:

- Meet for an hour for dinner, movie, or any other activity nearby.
- Take her home and seduce her. Have sex.

- Do some post-sex activities, such as eating, shopping, skating, going to the park, etc (if you want to see her again its a major bonus)

This is how an ideal date should go. And if you really hit it off with her, you will have many more dates, and ultimately a serious relationship with her.

Dealing with flakes

You set up the date, time and place. Five minutes before you leave, she cancels. Or even worse you arrive, wait for two hours and she never shows. This can happen! The main reason for a woman flaking is a lack or comfort and connection with you. Don't rush or pressure her into meeting you or going somewhere with you. You need to build it up, small steps of investment from her to you. Make her feel like she suggested it and she is chasing you. You can test the waters by throwing suggestions out there or even sending out cold offers such as. Oh I am at this awesome new salad restaurant or just been to the beach. Even better, send her pictures. This will entice her and captivate her interest to joining you next time.

Avoiding the Friend Zone

During your courtship a lot of guys easily fall into the friend zone by not setting the right frame. If you are always her shoulder to cry on about other guys or whenever she tests you, you react the wrong way then you will fall into the friend zone. To avoid this, keep things man to woman. Use physical contact, ignore her tests and always lead. If she asks where to go, you decide always. If she acts dominating put her in her place. Don't be a weak push over.

Keeping track

When your dating multiple girls a week it's a good idea to keep a track of who you are seeing. List their names in a spreadsheet and what the status of your relationship is with them. When did you last see them, what is your next plan? If you have been on a few dates with one girl or didn't speak for a while then this will help with moving things forward and keeping your mind clear.

Chapter 12: The Key to Flirting With Any Woman

According to many studies, interaction between humans is 80% physical, 20% words. You can use this massively to your advantage in the dating game. Since the physical signals we send make up such a huge part of the message we send then we must address these first.

Posture

Emotion is highly influenced by how we position ourselves and it also sends out a powerful message to people around us. Stand out in a positive way. Have your shoulders slightly back, chest out and legs shoulder width apart. When sitting, sit up straight and hold your head up high. When you walk maintain this strong frame plus some swagger. Your balls should lead you. Walk slowly and look cool, strong and confident. Hold eye contact and smile at the people who walk past you.

Gesturing

When you are talking use gestures to amplify your message. Be careful not to overdo this, you don't want to look like a clown. Check out some of the masters of public speaking for how they gesture. Observe videos of people like Barack Obama, Conor Mcgregor, Russell Brand and other famous charismatic people. Avoid touching your face too much, or any odd body language. Negative body language such as crossing your arms or defensive positioning should be avoided too. It is a great idea to film yourself talking or to attend public speaking courses such as toastmasters to see what your flaws are and improve them.

Eye Contact

Have a good balance of eye contact. Don't stare or look at the floor too long. Hold the person's gaze when you are talking and look away to give them space when thinking. If you want to increase intensity you can stare a little longer. This is great for silences with a girl.

Touching

A good friend of mine is a highly successful salesman. A powerful tool I have seen him use is touching. Now and then he will tap your arm or leg or wherever to grab your attention. He particularly does this when you break eye contact. It is a great way to keep you engaged. With a women you can take it further with kino escalation which is a seduction tool used to physically escalate on women in a smooth way. More on that later. You can build comfort with her by making excuses to touch her such as looking at her tattoos or jewelry.

Words

Paint pictures with the language you use. Women are highly emotional and will be turned on by this kind of language. Say things that create images and feelings in her mind such as. Instead of saying I went on an awesome surf trip. Say I went surfing and it was such a thrill, blue waves crashing over me in the depth of the sea. Or instead of yeah that movie was sick. Say, that movie made me really feel inspired by the struggle of the character and the love he felt for his wife. Another example, last weekend i went hiking, it was so cold. It becomes, last weekend I went on this adventure into the valley, you could see the sun bursting through the mountains and there was this chill in the air, it was such a mystical adventure. You get the vibe.

Tonality

Avoid being a monotone robot voice like most men. Try to bend the pitch of your ending sentences or on words that have an impact. Study the greats on YouTube such as comedians or politicians. You don't need to go overboard here, just mix it up a little to engage them. You can gauge their attention through level of eye contact and body language.

Let Her Talk

At the beginning of an interaction with a woman you should do most of the talking. Make assumptions and put her at ease. As the conversation progresses ask leading questions. Who, what, where, when and how. Get her to open up about herself and build attraction to you. Ask about her family, love life, dreams and ambitions. Talk about subjects that are highly emotional. Cover the subject of sex also. If you talk about yourself, do it in a positive way but don't brag. Tell stories that display your high value. Such as the time you rescued a cat or travelled to a new place alone. Avoid negative topics that can cause animosity such as religion, politics or race.

Lead

The whole time you should plant seeds in her mind for the future. Talk about things you could do together. Talk about your house, make her want to do these things and go to these places with you. Set the frame.

Chapter 13: Sex

Sex is a must in any relationship. It is the physical act of intimacy. It is an expression of love, trust, and devotion. This is why it is a deeper act when done by two individuals who love each other because it's not just about lust but also about connection and commitment.

However, sex in a relationship can become stale sometimes, especially after being together for a long time. It can become a routine and this is something that you should avoid. Sex should always be exciting even after being together for years. For it to be exciting, here are the things that you need to do.

Kino Escalation

I know this might be the first time that you have heard of this term. This is something that master seducers have long used and is a powerful seduction technique. It starts from the beginning to the dating set and lasts until the very end. And the level of intensity increases as the interaction with the girl progresses, thus the term 'escalation'. 'Kino' is just short for kinesthetics, or the physical touch between a man and a woman. The ultimate end of kino escalation, is of course, sex. And to reach this, you should first go through several levels of physical intimacy.

Building up intimacy is not really a requirement. Nothing is stopping you from going directly to sex if both you are up for it. However, gradually building up sexual tension is a lot more exciting than proceeding directly to sex. It is also more socially acceptable, not to mention classier and more calibrated.

Basic Principles

This technique won't work if you do not have **confidence**. This is why I always put emphasis on having confidence in yourself because you need it as you progress in the dating game. When touching the woman, whether it is touching her knee, giving her a hug, or giving her a kiss, you need to be confident in what you are doing. It should be deliberate and calm, as if it is the most natural thing in the world to do.

Awareness

A key principle of kino escalation. This means awareness of the signals that the woman sends. She might not say it upfront but she can be sending signals that you are going too far. She might turn her head slightly to one side when you come nearer or slowly shift her position to remove your hands from her knees. You need to back off a little because it means she is not yet ready. But do not be discouraged. If you play your cards right, you can still continue to escalate a little later. Just be aware of subtle signals that she might be sending.

Kino also follows the principle, **two steps forward, one step back**. Kino is not a step by step process. It is done unevenly and slowly for it to be more effective. If you are touching her knees and you can sense that she likes it, pull your hand away for a few minutes. Then put it back again. Pulling out kino when it is clear that she is enjoying it only makes her more receptive to your next advances. Make her want it even more.

You should also keep your touch light and feathery. Touching does not mean placing your hand on her knee without moving, as if you are just resting your hand there. Stroke her knee lightly, or gently move your thumb against her hand. Your movement should be light and fluid. No jerky movements, please, or the woman will be surprised and the air of seduction will be gone.

Early Kino

Since this is done when you first meet the girl, this only involves simple and casual physical contact such as touching her arm to get her attention or letting your body touch if you are in a crowded area. You can also tell her that you know how to do palm-reading so that you can touch her hand for a long time. Again you could also check out her jewelry, muscles or tattoos. You can also place your hand on the small of her back to guide her to the dance floor.

Mid Kino

After some time and you are already having deeper conversation with the girl, you can now escalate by using more deliberate physical contact, such as hugging, stoking her arm or knee. Look deep into her eyes, take her by the hand. You can also start kissing mid-set, if you think the girl is ready. Although if your outside don't get too carried away, women are highly emotional and she might regret going to far and not come back with you. If you leave enough left to her imagination then she is more likely to follow you home and want it more.

Seduction Kino

You are now bringing the whole process to a close. You and the girl are becoming more sexual at this point. This involves heavy kissing and groping, that will ultimately lead to sex. Again, only do the seduction-phase kino in a place where you can actually have sex. Believe me, it spoils the mood when you are both ready to do it but of course you can't because people might see you. When you have moved to the right location you can escalate more. Start with kissing, touching and then foreplay before leading towards sex. After sex make sure you hug her and attentive to her feelings. Don't be cold hearted and fall asleep or worse ask her to leave. Care for your woman.

Have Sex Goals

When having sex, you should have a goal that you want to achieve. You might say the big O or orgasm has always been the goal for having sex, right? Bringing pleasure to your partner and to yourself. Having sex is not just about achieving orgasm. It can be about a number of things. It can be for relaxation because sex relieves stress and tension. It can also be done for experimentation. You and your girlfriend might want to try something new and different, such as using kinky toys, costumes, etc. Couples also do it for emotional connection. This is why a lot of people have sex after a big fight because it makes them feel connected again.

Increase Your Sex Drive

To have great and exciting sex, you have to have the appetite for it. You can increase your libido or sex drive by eating healthy food, exercising, and taking libido inducers. Keep yourself stimulated by imaging her in different sexual situations. If you use pornography be careful not to let it take over. Watching a little now and then is great for inspiration but a lot of pornography is unrealistic and overly sexual. You may end up over stimulating your mind and then find it hard to be aroused by normal sex with a girl. There are also various over the counter supplements you can take for increasing sexual drive. Make sure you research them fully first.

Show Your Emotions

When having sex, do not be afraid to show your emotions. In fact, this is the perfect time to show your emotions because you are connecting to her on a primal level. Tell her how much you love her while kissing her or stroking her body. Or how much you find her beautiful and sexy. Girls are very self conscious during sex and it is the man's responsibility to put her at ease. Be loud and vocal, tell her she can do anything, ask her what she likes. Bring her out to the wild side.

Foreplay

Did you know that many women prefer foreplay than the actual penetration? In fact, a lot of them can achieve their orgasm via foreplay. The path to sex should be taken step by step. No rush, don't just jam it in there! Unless of course you are in a hurry or having adventurous outdoors sex.

Tease and pleasure her body. Learn about the things that make her orgasm. You will know this based on her reaction. Massage her breasts, go down on her. If you are good at what you are doing, you will also know when she is faking.

Talk Dirty

Another way to make sex more exciting is to talk dirty. You can do this not only when having sex but also when talking to her through chat or text or on the phone. The anticipation of what you are going to do to her when you are finally together will make her more excited to do the deed with you. When your having sex be very vocal about how you feel. Communication is a great tool to use during sex.

Maintain Eye Contact

Intense eye contact while having sex is a great turn on because it makes her feel that you are not just after her body and having sex with her. You are also trying to connect with her by looking into her eyes. And when having sex, looking at her will make her feel beautiful. This is especially effective when you are going down on her. And just looking at her reaction while pleasuring her is a big turn on by itself.

After Sex

Depending on your level of interest in the girl you should be aware of a few things. First and foremost regardless of your level of interest, be a gentleman. Hug her a little, tell her it was great. Let her take a shower first and if she has to leave, send her back or arrange transport. If you are looking for a relationship with the girl a great thing you can do to help it will be to go and eat together. This is a really girlfriend boyfriend thing to do and will have a massive impact on her impression of you.

Threesomes

If both of you are open to anything when it comes to sex, you can maybe try having a threesome. The trick here is to know if she is okay with it, and finding the third person. The third person can be a male or a female, depending on your preference. If she is intro threesomes, she probably knows someone who is also into it. Or maybe you also have friends who is into this kind of things. You'd be surprised at the number of people who want to have sex with two people at the same time.

You have to make her comfortable in expressing herself sexually. You can open the topic by innocently asking, have you ever considered having a threesome before? If her answer is a clear "hell no" then she is not into it and you shouldn't be forcing the issue. but if her reply is something vague, like "I'm not sure, I haven't really thought about it.." then it's possible that she might like it or that she actually likes it but is shy to admit it.

If you do decide to have a threesome and you already find the two lucky ladies (or it can be one lady and one guy) to do it with you, you need to take it slow, especially if one of you is new to this kind of thing. Set the mood right. You can also play a drinking game to make things more fun and at the same time to make everyone feel more relaxed.

Sex Addiction

Sex is a normal part of any adult person's life but did you know that there are people who are addicted to sex? And we all know that any form of addiction, and anything done in excess, is not good. You need to know the signs of sex addiction especially if you are venturing out in the dating world and meeting a lot of different people every day.

- Not performing well at work. Relationships with friends and family are impaired.
- Unplanned pregnancies and STDs.
- Spends money on prostitutes and porn.
- Always thinking about sex.

- Wants to stop but is unable to.
- Depression and anxiety.

You need to look out for these signs because you do not want to become involved with someone who is addicted to sex. Or worse, become that someone who is addicted to sex.

If you know someone who is addicted to sex or if you think you yourself are addicted to sex, you should seek help right away. Do not be embarrassed about it because I know a lot of people who have the same problem. You can go to a therapist or a counseling group to help you overcome your addiction. Here are some stories of people who were once addicted to sex but were able to overcome the addiction before they did something really terrible.

Take a look at these examples. Do they seem familiar?

Sheila has been to several serious relationships but she always cheats no matter how kind and loving her partner is. The main reason for her cheating is her addiction to sex. She just becomes bored after being with the same man for months. She knows she has a problem and wants it to stop. So she attended a group called Sex Addicts anonymous and she is now free from sex addiction for 3 years.

Many people think that having the perfect life won't lead to any form of addiction but they are wrong. Take Jude's case, for example. He had an attractive and supportive wife, two beautiful kids, a high-paying job, a large home, and basically anything that a man could ever hope for. The only problem is he also has sex addiction. And it is a secret. He pays prostitutes and has sex with them regularly. Until he got caught. It ruined his life. When his wife found out about his sex addiction, she immediately divorced him and she took the kids with her. He was too embarrassed to show his face to work so he also quit his job. He lost everything. He knows he has a problem and sought counseling. He visits a therapist regularly and attends a counseling group. Today, he is free from his sex addiction and is spending time with his wife and kids. They may not be back together again but at least they are in good terms and he can spend time with his children again.

Michelle is addicted to sex and she knows it and she loves it. She meets men almost every day and goes to their house or apartment to have sex. Until one day, she woke up after a hard night of partying and drinking, in the hospital, with bruises all over her body. She was beaten and raped. By whom, she is not sure because she can barely remember the events of the night before. She was lucky someone saw her lying near the dumpster and she was brought to the hospital. Michelle's solution is to seek help from professionals and people who have had the same experience as her. She is now 5 years clean and is a volunteer to her local Sex Addicts Anonymous group.

Chapter 14: Make Your Girlfriend (or one of them)

I've been in a couple of serious relationships and I can say that I am well experienced. I have dated a lot of women but only a few became serious, my choice. For now, I really don't like any commitment and I prefer playing the field or to be in a open relationship. But if your goal is to really be in a serious relationship, then here is some useful advice that I can give you.

First and foremost, how can she become your girlfriend? You have to look at it from a female's perspective. Something becomes more desirable for women when other women also want it. For most guys this might seem like counterintuitive advice. Remember women are highly emotional and we have to view the situation from their perspective. This means that the more girls want you, the higher your chances are of making her your girlfriend. Women like the competition and the chase, with you as their reward. This is why you need to keep things exciting. Do not just give her anything she wants. Let her know that you have other choices. Make her wait for your texts and be vague with your answers. She will then become almost addicted to you and would want nothing more than to be your girlfriend.

When you are finally together, you shouldn't be like those guys who stop going out with their guy friends just because they now have a girlfriend. Girlfriends may come and go, but guy friendships last forever. Unless you do something to ruin it, such as ignoring your friends because you are in a relationship now. Do not let your world revolve around the girl. Don't give her your all. Do not make the same mistake that I did. Or you will end up with nothing once the relationship turns sour. I am living proof of this. Neglecting my life for my girl was so extreme for me that I had to move to a new area and start fresh. Don't miss out on the rest of your life.

Make Your Life Interesting

Learning new hobbies or changing your lifestyle is attractive. Your girlfriend will fall even more in love with you because you continue making yourself even more interesting. Moreover, if you have an interesting life outside of your relationship, you will not end up becoming a needy and clingy boyfriend because you do not feel bored when your girlfriend is busy. Believe me, this is the only solution. Tell her that you are looking forward to seeing her after you go meet some friends.

Keep seducing your woman and grow your relationship. However, just because you are in a relationship with her already does not mean you should go easy on your seduction techniques. Remember that relationships require work and if you want to keep the fire burning, you have to **keep seducing her**, which means that you still have to use the techniques that you have learned in the previous chapters. Just remember to **keep the skill** alive at all times. Make her more invested in the relationship and let her be the chaser instead of the other way around. Don't act needy and be afraid of the relationship failing. You can always start over now that you know the way to play.

Take The Lead

Although both of you should call the shots in your relationship, you need to become the leader in most aspects of it. Be responsible for her and make her feel safe, protected, and secured. And when in a relationship, do not forget to always be a gentleman by giving her compliments and being romantic especially when there is a special occasion like her birthday or your anniversary.

Make it Real

When you are together, make every second being with her count. You should not be in a relationship just for the sake of having a girl by your side or just to show her off to your friends. After all, you are just wasting both of your time if you know you are not that into her. you might just end up hurting her in the end, and this is not something that I encourage because we should love girls and not make them cry.

Develop Your Emotions

Have more empathy and vulnerability. Girls are suckers for men who show their emotional side. This does not mean that you should go crying to your girl whenever you have a problem. However, showing her that you are human and you also have a soft side is always a plus in any relationship. Letting out this emotional side of yours is helpful because it makes you more relatable to your girlfriend. Besides, bottling up all those emotions because that's how a man should act is so midcentury. You have to catch up with the times and understand that men are now allowed to have a soft side.

Look at guys like Justin Bieber or a lot of Asian celebrities, they have a very feminine side but are highly attractive to many women. It's important to note here that each culture you come across, the girls will respond differently. For example Asian girls often prefer feminine, skinny cute guys. Whilst latino or Eastern European women love alpha males who are muscular and dominant.

Set The Frame

Another technique that you should still be using when in a relationship is to set the frame. And the right kind of frame when in this situation is honesty. Of course you should really be honest by not doing things that will break her trust but you should also frame yourself as an honest person especially if she has trust issues because of her past relationships. Tell her what you are looking for in a relationship. Maybe your happy being single or looking to meet new people. If you are in a committed relationship have trust and honesty. To do this, you have to be open with her at all times. Tell her where you are going, who you are going out with, etc. Some men may think this is too much but if you really want to gain her trust, you have to do this. Later on, once she fully trusts you, she won't need such details and reassurances whenever you go out without her. You should also trust her, you don't want to be checking up on her all the time. Give her the trust, often women will respect that. If they don't move on and don't be jaded by the experience.

Strive To Be Better

Not just you but also her. You need to work on your relationship if you want it to last long. It is not just about the right game but also about commitment and completely loving the other person no matter what. Always go out on dates and do things together. Keep the magic and excitement alive.

Open Relationships

Maybe the standard monogamous relationship isn't for you, it certainly isn't my preferred choice. I prefer to be open in a relationship and see other women as I please. If this is also your preference then it needs to be framed right at the start. Let the woman you know early on that this is how you like to be. You can say something like. I am a really busy person and I don't have time to commit to a serious relationship right now. I really like you and am happy to see you as much as possible without the pressure of us being in a serious relationship. We can see other people if we want. She will respect you for telling her this instead of being a low value guy that lies and manipulates. If she isn't cool with it, that is fine. Move on and find someone who is.

Chapter 15: Lifestyle Hacks

There is much more to improving your appearance and your pickup game that can help you attract women effortlessly. Improving on the following aspects of yourself will help you to become an alpha male.

Personal development should be a pillar of your journey not just in meeting women but in your life. Have goals that you want to achieve on the long, short and mid term. Constantly review them and make plans to achieve them. Take full responsibility and self awareness for your personal development.

Have an abundance of resources. You will not be able to function well if you do not have enough resources to begin with. I quit my office job and became a DJ because this job pays better. Meeting beautiful women here and there in my job is a huge bonus, too. You should also learn how to manage your finances well. Do not fall into the trap of acquiring debt just to impress women. Being able to take care of yourself and having the comfort to take a girl out will put you at ease. This isn't about being a provider and taking care of a woman financially. Rather its about affording the lifestyle with ease that will attract and put you into contact with high quality women.

Relationships

I'm not just talking about relationships with women but also with other people in your life such as your family and friends. Maybe you have unsettled arguments or bad feelings with people. Do your best to be the better man and resolve them. Improving your relationships can help you become a better person. It will raise your self esteem, making you feel better about yourself and leading to more romantic success.

Fatherhood

If you already have a child but your relationship with the mother didn't go well, you should make sure that you are a good father to your child. Take responsibility, provide for and see your child regularly. Women find this attractive because it shows you have a sense of responsibility. Don't try to hide that you have children. Most women will be fine with it.

Appearance

Always look presentable especially when going out and meeting women. Try to stay fit by working out regularly and eating healthy food. Wear clothes that fit nicely, get a good haircut and shave regularly. Every month or two you should update your fashion. This will do wonders for your confidence.
If you want women to notice you, you should start dressing in a more fashionable way especially when going out at night. Choose clothes that fit nicely and that accentuate your assets. Know how to dress a little more sexually. Instead of buttoning up your shirt all the way to your neck, why not unbutton a couple buttons to make yourself look more relaxed and comfortable? You can also wear clothes that bring out the masculine features of your body. Women will surely fall all over themselves when they see how hot and sexual you are. Accessorize where possible, you don't need a rolex or bling bling, often times something with a story and emotion behind it is way more powerful. Maybe you have a shark tooth bracelet taken from a Hawaii surf trip or a bracelet from a rock concert. These are great conversation starters.

Home

If you still live with your parents you might want to think about moving out to your own place. It will make things a lot more comfortable for the girls. You should also aim to live in a decent area that is frequented by lots of hot women. That way you will encounter much more in your day to day life. Your home should be clean tidy and ready for a woman. Keep some candles, wine and music at easy access for when they visit. You can also buy some board games or activities to use as excuses for a woman to come over or to keep them entertained.

Lifestyle

Go out every week. Attend events, concerts and meet ups. Learn new things and have cool hobbies. Meet your friends. Travel to new places. Have a bucket list. Make your life more interesting and the women will flow to you. The more out there you are the more likely you are to meet a great woman.

Have More Fun

Do not think that you need to carry the weight of the world on your shoulders. Although it is important to take certain things seriously, you must still remember to have fun if you want to make women see you as someone who is fun to be with. Learn to be funny and improve your sense of humour, it is dynamite with the ladies. You can watch comedians and funny movies online to get a better understanding of how to be funny.

Be Confident

I cannot stress this enough because confidence is like the key to everything. It can lead you to a lot of great things. Remove all self-doubt and start thinking positively about yourself. If others can do it, so can you. To become more confident is to overcome more of your fears. If you fear talking strangers or public speaking for example you need to take more action to overcome it. Talk to more strangers, do some presentations. Have greater self awareness to constantly identify your fears and figure out ways to overcome them. Again journaling and meditation will help this massively. If you have deeper issues, consider seeing a psychologist.

Bonus Chapter: The Quick System

Whether you are trying to attract women in a club at night, at the park in the morning, or online. The Quick System has helped a lot of men secure dates and relationships in the past and is proven to be effective. It is like the summary, or the condensed version, of all dating strategies that successful alpha males use, which is why it is called Quick!

It is important that you know what you need to do before you take action. You cannot just go to the girl while your fingers are crossed tightly behind your back. This is not the right time to put everything on fate or luck. You should have a plan, like this system specially devised for men who are at a loss like you.

Let's assume that you have already identified your target. What will be your next step? Use the guide below as your plan of attack.

Intent

You have seen this before, done by not only men but also women. The guy keeps throwing glances at the girl. Please do not stare unless you want the girl to think you are creepy! Just look at her with intent, meaning you have a purpose for looking at her. And what would that purpose be? You want to meet her or talk to her. By looking at her, you are making her aware of your presence. You are also letting her know that you are checking her out in an admiring way and not a creepy stalker kind of way. And while doing this, expect that the reaction will be good so that good fortune will come your way. You can look for indicators of interest from her such as eye contact or a smile. Gesture back to her in a fun way.

Find an Excuse

Any excuse will do. The music/food/place/etc. is great. Have you tried this/that before? This reminds me of.... Have we met before? What do you recommend. This is also not the time to be completely honest. Do not say, "Hey I've been checking you out and I like what I'm seeing. Can we go to my place later? "No matter how hot, gorgeous, or irresistible you think you are, you will still get a hard slap on your face if you say this to any girl you meet for the first time. Also, if the girl is with a group of girls, why not start a conversation with all of them. Who knows, you might end just hit it off with one of the girls. Remember that life is too short and you better be spending it trying to attract girls because volume of girls to attract is huge. So many girls, so little time, they say.

Once The Opening Statement Has Been Said, Have Fun

You do not need to go there with a scripted conversation in mind. Her responses might not be what you are imagining. You need to be able to sustain an interesting conversation as naturally as possible. This is why having fun while doing this is important. If you are not having fun, then a conversation that sounds natural is difficult to achieve. Just let loose, let yourself go, and go with the flow.

Use Emotional Spiking

Emotional spiking is done during a conversation. This is what makes conversations interesting. Boring or lukewarm conversation is the worst thing that can happen to you while talking to a girl. Negative is better than lukewarm. Play on the girl's emotions while talking to her. Talking about the weather or what she eats in the morning, or any mundane topic won't make her feel excited. Talk about getting a tattoo, travelling to exotic places, or anything that will elicit an extreme reaction from the girl. You do not necessarily need to agree to everything the girl is saying because the conversation will be too boring. Opposing views and opinions make great conversations.

You need to speak to her as naturally as possible (not like an interrogation). Here's how it should go: start with a qualifying question (Have you ever thought of having a tattoo?), challenge her reply (If she says no, ask her why not?), hold the intensity (If she says tattoos do not look good as one gets older, you can say she's wrong because you have seen a lot of old women sporting a tattoo and they look cool), and finally, release the intensity or give reward (You can say she later on that she has a point, although you still believe women with tattoos look hot).

Find Out More About Her

The conversation shouldn't be just about using strategies to get in her pants, although it should be one of your agendas. Of course, you should have the genuine interest to find out more about her. Again, do not sound like an interviewer by asking her about her favorite color, birthday, work experience, educational background. Pretty soon she'll ask you if you just want her to give you her CV. This is also the right time to share a little about yourself. If you open up a little, she will also be more willing to share about herself. Just be careful not to make it all about you. This may not be the time yet to share secrets but you are getting there.

However, this is the perfect time to use sexual framing-- the secret ingredient to seduction. I swear by this because it works ALL. THE. TIME. It is not enough that you are a great-looking person who has everything going for you. You should also know how to market yourself to your target audience, so to speak.

While you are getting to know each other, drop comments here and there that forms your sexual frame. There are several ways to frame sex. For example, commenting about sexual morals, purity, or respectability is not a good frame if you want to bring the lady home with you on your first night. On the other hand, if you say statements that imply you are not a judgmental person and you are turned on by women who are not afraid to show their sexual desires, then you will surely end up sleeping with her in the same bed. You should also pay attention to your gestures. Being relaxed and letting yourself loose will surely send the right message to the girl instead of acting all proper. Touch her arms, hair, even knees or legs when you think she is ready. Believe me, sexual framing does wonders even to the least attractive guys.

Move In For The Kill

Okay, this sounds like a tip for a hunter but isn't dating a lot like hunting? It is easy if the girl is all by herself because you can just simply make your move without thinking about other people. If she is with a group of friends, however, then you need to do it a little differently, especially if she is with a group of girlfriends. You do not want to make the other girls feel unattractive because you chose only one of them, right? Charm them also, they will then feel comfortable about letting her go with you. This is much easier if you are with your guy friends who can act as your wingmen. Maybe they can keep the other girls occupied while you do your thing with your target. You can also just ask her to dance if you are at a club or walk or jog alongside her if you are outside.

Close it With Sex

Whether you like to admit it or not, the ultimate goal of approaching a woman is, of course, because you like her but also because you want to get in her pants. Lucky you if you are able to do it on the same day that you met her. How can you close the conversation with sex? You cannot simply say, so would you like to have sex with me, after asking her about her life, unless you want a big slap on your face. You have to segue smoothly. This is where sexual framing leads to. If you frame sex, well, sexually enough, then your conversation with the woman will end here 100 percent. The conversation should build up in such a way that both of you, especially her, would want to end up in each other's arms (and in the same bed). Leading her is also a key component. Get her invested by moving her around different locations. Or if she seems really into you, lead her home.

So how to move into a more intimate topic like sex? At this point in your interaction, you are already past the small talk. You should already be asking questions like "what do you find attractive in a guy?", "do you still remember your first kiss? or "would you sleep with someone on the first date if the connection is strong enough?" Questions like these will make her less feel shy about expressing herself sexually, and will make her not afraid to have sex with you.

Use kino escalation to smoothly escalate on her physically. Put on some sexy music and lead her. Start kissing and gradually move towards more sexual intimacy and then sex. After sex be a gentleman and use girlfriend techniques discussed earlier.

Following this system down to a tee is not the only thing that you should do, if you want to become an alpha male who attracts women the way a rotten fruit attracts flies. Or the way a fragrant flower attracts bees, if you want a better-sounding metaphor. Another really important and must-do tip is to know what you want in a girl, or a girlfriend. And how to become a man that girls want, and more specifically, how to become the man that the type of girl you want wants? You can see more about this in the early chapter. Be sure to take action on the advice.

You cannot just go up to every girl you see and want her to become your girlfriend. That would be a turn off. As I have mentioned before, you should not be wasting your time on women whom you are not attracted to or you do not have any strong connection with. Have a mindset of abundance. There are so many women out there that would date you.

Again, this does not mean that you should be a douche to the rest of the girls who do not meet your "standards". You should still be able to make all the girls you meet feel attractive but your special efforts should be saved for those that you really like.

Likewise, you should not expect girls to like you back if you do not do anything to improve yourself, if you remain the shy and unconfident man that you are who has nothing to show for himself. You need to take actions if you want to be an attractive man who always attract girls wherever he goes.

Conclusion

There you have it, a full guide to take you from zero to hero. Maybe you have just come out of a long term relationship or maybe you are just starting out. You could even be an advanced player. Wherever you are at in your journey if you follow the advice before and adapt it to your life then you will surely see results. Remember that it is a journey, just because you got laid or ended up with a relationship doesn't mean that you should stop developing. Live a balanced life of health, wealth, passions, career and romance. Keep the spark alive in your love life and keep improving.

I suggest that you read this book more than once and highlight the things that stick out to you. The dating game is an ongoing journey and things you first read might not be apparent to you then but will be more relevant later on. Keep track of your progress, your dates, your highs, your lows. Set goals for what you want and take action. If your self aware then your more likely to get what you want.

If you are anywhere near as low as I was when starting out then believe me it gets better. The responsibility for that is with you. Don't expect an overnight transformation. It takes times. Sometimes you will go out for weeks and months with no result but taking part is what will prepare you for when you have the right opportunities.

Maybe a complete overhaul of your life is what you need. It was for me. Change your location, travel, make new friends and follow a new path. Develop yourself and evolve to a new you.

Who you were before is not going to determine who you are destined to be.

Follow the advice and stay persistent.

Thank You

If you enjoyed this book please check out my other books on and stay up to date with us at Chase Attraction on Facebook and Instagram.

Thanks for Reading!

What Did You Think of, **Make Her Chase You: The Simple Strategy to Attract Women**

I know you could have picked any number of books to read, but you picked this book and for that I am extremely grateful.

I hope that it added at value and quality to your everyday life. If so, it would be really nice if you could share this book with your friends and family by posting to Facebook and Twitter.

If you enjoyed this book and found some benefit in reading this, I'd like to hear from you and hope that you could take some time to post a review. Your feedback and support will help this author to greatly improve his writing craft for future projects and make this book even better.

I want you, the reader, to know that your review is very important and so, if you'd like to leave a review, all you have to do is click here and away you go. I wish you all the best in your future success!

Darcy Carter 2018

Buyer Bonus

I want to thank you for your purchase of this book. As a way of extending my thanks I am giving you full access to exclusive resources, including:

- Free courses and books
- Building a lifestyle that will guarantee you success with women
- How to Look and Feel Your Best
- Keep the conversation going, without appearing awkward
- How to confidently express yourself and captivate attention
- And much more about confidence, relationships and dating

Free Sign Up Here

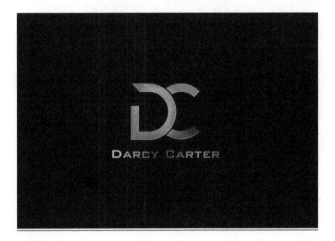